LANGUAGE ONE

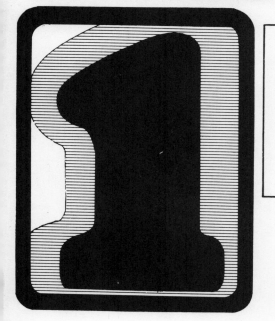

**SADLER
HAYLLAR
POWELL**

M

First published 1977 by
THE MACMILLAN COMPANY OF AUSTRALIA PTY LTD
107 Moray Street, South Melbourne 3205
6 George Place, Artarmon 2064
Reprinted 1978 (twice), 1979 (three times), 1980 (twice)

Associated companies in
London and Basingstoke, England
New York Dublin Johannesburg Delhi

National Library of Australia
cataloguing in publication data
Sadler, Rex Kevin.
    Language one.

    ISBN 0 333 23002 7
    1. English language — Composition and exercises.
    I. Hayllar, Thomas Albert S., joint author.
    II. Powell, Clifford J., joint author. III. Title.

372.6076

Set in Baskerville and Helvetica by The Markby Group
Printed in Hong Kong by
Wing King Tong Co Ltd

Contents

Preface

In the last ten years there has been a drift away from the study of formal language skills in English. The drift began when it was discovered that students were *never* in the mood for the subjunctive, and that much of parsing and analysis was irrelevant to contemporary speech and writing. Educators perceived that too much formal work was 'killing' English, in the sense that students were completing courses with a fairly thorough grounding, but at the same time with very little interest or enjoyment. The twin charges of 'irrelevance' and 'stifling interest', laid at the door of formal language, were enough to start teachers on the task of revising their teaching approaches. The drift was on, and English courses moved away from formal language into more creative, experiential fields.

Unfortunately things went too far. The noun was thrown out with the gerund. A generation of students grew up with little understanding of the foundations of English, and though their interest may have been high, their linguistic competence was, all too often, alarmingly low.

It is time now for our whole approach to the teaching of English to be taken back to the drawing board for further assessment.

Language One offers what we believe to be a balanced approach in this area of English, with appeal for both teachers and students. We have aimed at presenting a relevant study of English grammar and traditional language skills, and at the same time capturing student interest through the literary extracts and creative exercises used in the book.

Distinctive features of *Language One* include the following:

- Each unit commences with a passage from which the language work derives. Too many previous texts have offered an initial passage, and followed with an arbitrary 'bits 'n' pieces' presentation of language.

- All passages are contemporary, ranging in scope from suspense to humour, from shark attacks to shoes, from *Watership Down* to *Woman's Day*. Each passage is chosen for its high level of student interest.
- Units focus on traditional skills areas, such as comprehension, vocabulary extension, punctuation, spelling, creative writing and speech work. A wide variety of student exercises based on these areas is included.
- *Language One* contains its own student's reference dictionary at the back of the book.
- The format throughout is based on the best learning principles available to us from research. These include:
  - (a) material presented in small steps;
  - (b) opportunity for active responding by students;
  - (c) opportunity for feedback to students (through the marking of exercises);
  - (d) opportunity for the mastery of skills through practice.

The book is designed to be worked through, unit by unit, with the exception of Unit Nineteen, which offers topics for composition and creative writing.

We offer *Language One*, then, as the first book in a series, designed to teach the basics necessary for skilful use of the English language in an enjoyable way. There is plenty of work here for the student, but we make no apology for that. There are no shortcuts to competence.

Acknowledgements

The authors and publishers are grateful to the following for permission to reproduce copyright material.

Angus and Robertson Publishers and Rex Collings Ltd for 'A near miss' from *Watership Down* by Richard Adams © Rex Collings 1972; Progress Press, Moorabbin for 'Bondi of all places!' by Bruce Raymond from *Backdoor*, issue 9, 1976; Wilhelm Johnen and William Kimber & Co. Ltd for *Duel under the stars*; John Fairfax & Sons Ltd for 'Night of the Mustang' by Robert Mayne, *Sydney Morning Herald*, March 20, 1971; Angus & Robertson Publishers for 'Ben Hall — Bushranger' from *Ben Hall* by Frank Clune; News Ltd for 'The world in 200 years' from the *Daily Mirror*, April 6th, 1977; Macmillan Publishing Co. Inc. for *The germ killer* by John Mann, copyright © 1966; Collins Publishers for 'Elephants of the Congo' from *On Safari* by Armand Denis; Peter Wickham and *Stern* Magazine for 'Girl against the jungle' by Juliane Koepcke; The executors of the Ernest Hemingway estate and Jonathan Cape Ltd for 'The big fish' from *The Old Man and the Sea* by Ernest Hemingway; Mort Singer and the *Saturday Evening Post* for 'Dear Shoe' by Mort Singer; Hodder & Stoughton Children's Books for 'The points of the horse' from *Riding* by C. E. G. Hope; E. C. Publications Inc. for 'Teenager care' by Larry Siegel and Bob Clarke from *Mad Special* No. 10, copyright © 1969; the *Australian Women's Weekly* for 'Tips to safeguard your house' from 'How to survive a bushfire' by Sean Moylan; Oxford University Press for 'The wrong killer' from *The Man-eating Leopard of Rudraprayag* by Jim Corbett; Charles Boag for 'Light gone all dark', published in *Woman's Day*, September 2nd, 1974; Herman Wouk for an extract from *The 'Caine' Mutiny*; Brian Rodger and Rigby Ltd for 'A shark tried to eat me' from *Shark Hunters*.

Inga Moore, pp. 2-3, 6, 46, 76, 90; Chris Payne, pp. 5, 17, 29-31, 49, 51, 59, 107, 112-114, 117, 122, 126, 128-30, 133, 152, 157, 159-161, 170, 186; Herald & Weekly Times Ltd, pp. 11, 12, 25, 41, 106, 142, 185; Fox Photos, p. 11; John Trichen, p. 13; John Strane (Marineland), p. 43; Australian Broadcasting Commission, p. 63; IN-Bild, FOTO INTER NATIONES, p. 73; Central Press Photos, p. 74; South African Airways and the South African Tourist Corporation, p. 97; Pix Features, p. 106; News Ltd, p. 185; Carnation Co. Pty Ltd, p. 131; Alan Foley Pty Ltd, pp. 32, 144, 145, 151, 192, 194; Ken Done, p. 198; Clinton Research, p. 84; Uncle Ben's of Australia, p. 81, Anne Paterson, p. 96; Volvo Australia Pty Ltd, p. 199; Noel Hill, p. 197; *Sydney Morning Herald*, p. 176; American Express, p. 69; Russel McPhedran, pp. 120-121.

Unit One: Rabbit

Watership Down, by Richard Adams, is a sensitively written novel telling of the struggle of a group of rabbits to establish their own warren in new country. It has been widely acclaimed as a classic of animal literature.

In this extract, two of the rabbits have raided a nearby farm, hoping to free some domesticated rabbits held there.

A near miss

Suddenly Pipkin spoke from the floor. 'Hazel, there's a cat in the yard outside!'

'We're not afraid of cats,' said Hazel to Boxwood, 'as long as we're in the open.' Trying to appear unhurried, he went back to the floor by way of the straw-bale and crossed over to the door. Pipkin was looking through the hinge. He was plainly frightened.

'I think it's smelt us, Hazel,' he said. 'I'm afraid it knows where we are.'

'Don't stay there, then,' said Hazel. 'Follow me close and run when I do.' Without waiting to look out through the hinge, he went round the half-open door of the shed and stopped on the threshold.

The cat, a tabby with white chest and paws, was at the farther end of the little yard, walking slowly and deliberately along the side of a pile of logs. When Hazel appeared in the doorway it saw him at once and stood stock-still, with staring eyes and twitching tail. Hazel hopped slowly across the threshold and stopped again. Already sunlight was slanting across the yard and in the stillness the flies buzzed about a patch of dung a metre or two away. There was a smell of straw and dust and hawthorn.

'You look hungry,' said Hazel to the cat. 'Rats getting too clever, I suppose?'

The cat made no reply. Hazel sat blinking in the sunshine. The cat crouched almost flat on the ground, thrusting its head forward between its front paws. Close behind, Pipkin fidgeted and Hazel, never taking his eyes from the cat, could sense that he was trembling.

'Don't be frightened, Hlao-roo,' he whispered. 'I'll get you away, but you must wait till it comes for us. Keep still.'

The cat began to lash its tail. Its hindquarters lifted and wagged from side to side in mounting excitement.

'Can you run?' said Hazel. 'I think not. Why, you pop-eyed, back-door saucer-scraper —'

The cat flung itself across the yard and the two rabbits leapt into flight with great thrusts of their hind legs. The cat came very fast indeed and although both of them had been braced ready to move on the instant, they were barely out of the yard in time. Racing up the side of the long barn, they heard the Labrador barking in excitement as it ran to the full extent of its rope. A man's voice shouted to it. From the cover of the hedge beside the lane they turned and looked back. The cat had stopped short and was licking one paw with a pretence of nonchalance.

'They hate to look silly,' said Hazel. 'It won't give us any more trouble. If it hadn't charged at us like that it would have followed us much farther and probably called up another as well. And somehow you can't make a dash unless they do it first. It's a good thing you saw it coming, Hlao-roo.'

'I'm glad if I helped, Hazel. But what were we up to, and why did you talk to the rabbits in the box?'

'I'll tell you all about it later on. Let's go into the field now, and feed; then we can make our way home as slowly as you like.'

RICHARD ADAMS, *Watership Down*

Check your understanding

1 Hazel tried to appear unhurried crossing to the door because
   (a) he wanted to make a big impression on Boxwood.
   (b) he knew that rabbits didn't need to fear cats.
   (c) he knew that, if he showed fear, Pipkin's fear might turn to panic.
2 What effect did the appearance of Hazel have on the cat?
3 Choose the word closest in meaning to each of the following words from the passage.
   (a) threshold: grip, entrance, floor-board, brick
   (b) dung: manure, mud, rubbish, bags
   (c) braced: alert, watchful, supported, wide-eyed
   (d) nonchalance: annoyance, indifference, humour.
4 Explain why Hazel spoke to the cat.
5 'Hlao-roo' is another name for
   (a) the cat   (b) Hazel   (c) Pipkin   (d) Boxwood
6 Which word best describes the manner in which Hazel spoke to the cat?
       humorously   lazily   nervously
       insultingly   carefully
7 Though Hazel spoke to the cat, it did not answer him. The most likely reason for this is that
   (a) it was lost for words.
   (b) it didn't understand what Hazel said.
   (c) its only concern was to catch the rabbits.
   (d) cats are unable to talk.
8 Imagine that you were a bystander when the chase began. What two noises did you hear, apart from the noise of the chase?
9 Select *two* correct answers. Hazel wanted the cat to make a charge because
   (a) it would otherwise have had the energy to pursue them much further.
   (b) the rabbits were skilled at dodging.
   (c) he wanted to make a fool of it.
   (d) he knew it would help them make their dash.

10 Find at least two pieces of evidence to support the view that Hazel is clearly the leader of these rabbits.

NOUNS

A noun is a **naming** word. It is a word used to name

- **people:** George Washington, Michelle, Ed McGurk
- **places:** Sydney, Ayers Rock, Rio de Janeiro
- **objects:** sugar, horse, *Watership Down*, mountain, germ
- **qualities:** healthiness, folly, lunacy, generosity

Noun track-down

11 Rewrite these sentences in your workbook, filling in the blank spaces by choosing nouns from the brackets.
  (a) The [.....] were lucky to escape the [.....] by the [.....]. [charge, cat, rabbits]
  (b) The tame [.....] were kept in a [.....] by the [.....]. [farmer, rabbits, hutch].
  (c) A few [.....] can seem like [.....] when you are about to be attacked by an [.....]. [seconds, enemy, eternity]
  (d) [.....] said to [.....], 'We'd better take [.....] to avoid any [.....] on the [.....] back [.....].' [way, Hazel, care, Pipkin, home, danger]
  (e) The whole [.....] served as a [.....] to the two [.....]. [warning, intruders, incident]

12 In the following sentences, all the nouns have been printed in bold black type. Write each one in your workbook, and state whether it is the name of a **person (animal)**, **place**, **object** or **quality**.

(a) '**Hazel,** there's a **cat** in the **yard** outside!'

(b) Trying to appear unhurried, he went back to the **floor** by **way** of the **straw-bale** and crossed over to the **door.**

(c) **Pipkin** was looking through the **hinge.**

(d) **Hazel** hopped slowly across the **threshold** and stopped again.

(e) Already **sunlight** was slanting across the **yard** and in the **stillness** the **flies** buzzed about a **patch** of **dung** a **metre** or two away.

(f) Racing up the **side** of the long **barn,** they heard the **Labrador** barking in **excitement** as it ran to the full **extent** of its **chain.**

(g) A **man's voice** shouted to it.

(h) The **cat** had stopped short and was licking one **paw** with a **pretence** of **nonchalance.**

13 Pick out the nouns from among the following words used in the extract. (Where you are not sure, check back to see if the word is used as a naming word.) Write each one down in your workbook and state whether it is the name of a person, place, object or quality.

afraid	Boxwood	long
pile	Hlao-roo	stock-still
hawthorn	no	front
hindquarters		pop-eyed
braced	great	yard
dash	into as	trouble

half-open shed   saucer-scraper

eyes   staring racing thrusts

close   I'll the

Singular and plural of nouns

● When a noun stands for just **one** person, place, object or quality, that noun is said to be **singular** in number.

               cow   road   bus

● When a noun stands for **two or more** people, places, objects or qualities, that noun is said to be **plural** in number.

               cows   roads   buses

Most nouns in English form their plural by simply adding 's' to the singular form. For some nouns 'es' has to be added to the singular form.

14 Write out the words needed to fill the blank spaces in the following table.

	SINGULAR	PLURAL		SINGULAR	PLURAL
(a)	train	trains	(b)	.....	maps
(c)	glass	.....	(d)	shirt	.....
(e)	.....	envelopes	(f)	mattress	.....
(g)	.....	stones	(h)	singer	....
(i)	Peter	.....	(j)	smash	.....
(k)	Honda	.....	(l)	.....	mountains
(m)	tax	.....	(n)	.....	witches

15 The following nouns take irregular (unusual) plurals. Write down the plural form of each, if necessary looking the word up in a dictionary to find its plural form.

(a) hippopotamus	(b) tooth	(c) fish
(d) child	(e) goose	(f) foot
(g) calf	(h) sheep	(i) radius
(j) leaf	(k) wharf	(l) ox
(m) sheaf	(n) mouse	(o) knife
(p) loaf	(q) deer	(r) stadium
(s) thief	(t) louse	

The possessive form of nouns

The possessive form of a noun is used to indicate that the noun possesses, or owns, something.

Sam's shirt   the sun's rays

One aspect of nouns which causes a great deal of confusion is the use of the **apostrophe** (') to make the possessive form of a noun. Yet by learning three simple rules the difficulty is overcome.

- The singular possessive form of a noun is made by adding apostrophe 's' ('s) to the noun.
dog's leg
- The plural possessive form of a noun whose plural ends in 's' is made by adding only an apostrophe (').
dogs' legs
- The plural possessive form of nouns where the plural does not end in 's' is made by adding apostrophe 's' ('s).
children's toys

Look at these examples to refresh your mind on the rules. Then go ahead and do the exercises in your workbook, making the possessive forms of each noun.

the boot of the car   the car's boot
the cry of the birds   the birds' cry
the wool of all the sheep   all the sheep's wool

16 (a) the handbag of the lady   (b) the screech of the tyres
(c) the hands of the women   (d) the handbags of the ladies
(e) the books of the boys   (f) the window of the shop
(g) the pens of the girls   (h) the anger of the men
(i) the petals of the daisy   (j) the petals of the daisies
(k) the close of the day   (l) the trunk of the tree
(m) the edge of the cliff   (n) the noise of the trains
(o) the start of the season   (p) the feet of the mouse

MASTERING WORDS

17 Choose from each group of nouns the word closest in meaning to the first noun.

(a) dwelling: job, home, anchor, thought
(b) pelt: belt, fox, field, skin
(c) transformation: change, gallop, worship, move
(d) commotion: noise, group, adventure, prowler
(e) cluster: daze, hold, grapes, bunch
(f) competence: exercise, skilfulness, accident, competition
(g) gesture: face, hand, action, description
(h) placard: criminal, place, poster, food
(i) sequence: spangle, soldier, events, series
(j) tuition: piano, knowledge, teaching, guard

18 Use each word in a sentence to show that you understand its meaning. If necessary, consult your dictionary for help.

(a) similar	(b) souvenir	(c) antique
(d) prejudice	(e) hospitable	(f) weird
(g) dinghy	(h) reservoir	(i) dominate
(j) finance	(k) guarantee	(l) glamour
(m) livelihood	(n) essential	(o) forfeit
(p) orbit		

PUNCTUATION

19 A **capital letter** is used to start new sentences, and a **full stop** is used at the end of each completed sentence. Put capitals and full stops in the following passage where they are required.

his hands and knees were trembling slightly he wondered how long it would take at any moment he knew he would be discovered slowly they moved towards him suddenly they stopped the leader muttered something and they turned and began to walk away it was some minutes before he could trust himself to move

RABBIT WORD-SALAD

20   In the word-salad below there are twenty-five words which have some association with the world of rabbits. You'll find them in the salad only in straight lines, but they may be printed forwards or backwards, horizontally, vertically or diagonally. One word is already picked out in bold type, to serve as an example.

```
E  S  S  A  R  G  H  H  L  I  Z  P  S
O  Y  T  W  S  U  E  O  D  O  N  A  D
W  A  R  R  E  N  D  N  X  B  I  T  O
F  G  E  W  D  R  G  Q  E  U  J  C  O
W  G  A  P  S  G  E  L  D  N  I  H  W
O  P  M  F  U  R  C  W  N  N  V  O  M
L  L  E  T  T  U  C  E  R  Y  R  K  X
L  E  S  O  T  N  B  U  T  R  V  C  H
O  G  Z  R  J  S  T  K  J  L  B  U  Y
H  S  O  R  W  R  A  B  B  I  T  B  D
X  K  N  A  B  D  I  G  P  C  Y  J  Q
P  F  V  C  Z  N  L  O  H  N  M  S  A
```

THE WRITE APPROACH

Animals *do* feel things, and they *can* communicate with each other! There's no doubt about it! Maybe their communication is not quite as 'human' as the adult fantasy in the book by Richard Adams, but certainly it is there!

Try weaving your own fantasy around one of the following situations. Let your animals communicate with each other, and try to get your reader to experience their emotions.

21   A mother dingo is killed and her three pups are left to fend for themselves.

22   A wild stallion is caught and put into a corral with other brum-
     bies.

23   A monkey and his mates form a plan to get out of their cage at
     the zoo, and really have some fun.

TALK TIME

Use the following themes for class discussions.

24   'The *Watership Down* heroes are too human and not rabbity enough, or they are too rabbity and not human enough, or they are an excellent mixture of both.' Which do you agree with most?

25   We humans could learn more from the so-called 'lower' animals than we could from each other.

26   A well cared for, captive animal is better off than a free animal.

Unit Two: Surf

Bondi of all places!

I have ridden Waimea Bay a number of times, which would have to be considered the largest surfable surf spot in the world. However, I'd like to tell you about the largest wave I can remember riding here in Australia.

Surprisingly enough, it was at Bondi of all places. As usual, a large southerly storm created huge seas in the Sydney area. Actually, the only way you surf big waves in the Sydney area is when a storm is on. It was really really big, and Brad Mayes, Paul Manstead and I walked right around the roadway to the southern end of the point.

There were set waves breaking way out to sea in deep water. We thought we had timed it right with a safe lull, so we jumped off this big flat rock and started paddling like crazy.

Out of fear, I was paddling the fastest. As we approached the line-up area, these three waves were coming in to meet us. The first one was so huge that it seemed as if I was paddling up it for ages. Paddle, paddle, paddle.

I quickly focused my attention on the third wave that was just about to break, and I almost bailed out at the top, but decided to take the punt and try to get through, which I did.

As the wave went past me, my heart was going BOOM, BOOM, BOOM, and I said almost out loud . . . My God. How am I going to get in?

I turned around and saw how far out to sea I·was, and thought that maybe it would have been better to get washed in with my other two friends. They ended up getting washed up the rocks and scratched up a bit, along with their boards.

I picked this wave which would have been over four metres. I started going across the face in a right slide. I could see this giant left coming at me from the northern point.

I had to make this decision, as I was going across the top, whether I wanted to try and pull off one of these bounce-off-the-white-water things you do in small surf. It really looked perfect to try to do it . . . almost inviting me to try.

The moment of truth finally came where I could try it or pull out. But then I noticed that it had become too late, and I was committed.

I pulled it up and went up, up and away, and got terribly wiped out.

I still think about that one moment often, as it was really a big wave, and a situation that I'd like to come in contact with again.

BRUCE RAYMOND, *Backdoor*

Check your understanding

1 Which emotion does the title of this article intend to convey to the reader?
(a) anger (b) happiness (c) surprise (d) mystery

2 Which answer is correct? Waimea Bay
(a) has the largest waves in the world.
(b) has the biggest waves that can be surfed in the world.
(c) is the world's most popular surfing beach.
(d) is the world's most famous surfing beach.

3 Which is correct? The only way to surf big waves in Sydney is to
(a) wait for a southerly wind.
(b) go to Bondi.
(c) wait for a storm surf.
(d) catch the third wave in the set.

4 How did the writer explain the fact that he paddled faster than his mates?

5 Match the meaning in the right column with the word in the left column.

WORD	MEANING
(a) committed	a gamble
(b) lull	a wave that breaks away to the left side
(c) bailed out	a pause in the activity
(d) punt	unable to withdraw
(e) left	let go of the surfboard and try to get through the wave without it

6 Which is correct? As he was going over the third wave the writer wondered
(a) why he'd been so foolish.
(b) what would happen if he was washed on the rocks.
(c) what would happen if another wave came.
(d) how he would ever get in.

7   The writer thought he might have done better to get washed in with his friends because
(a)   they only got scratched a little.
(b)   he was so far out to sea.
(c)   he didn't like being on his own.
(d)   he knew he would probably be wiped out.

8   Why did the writer attempt the difficult manoeuvre?

9   Explain in your own words the meaning of 'wiped out'.

10   In your own words, tell why the writer would like to go through the same situation again. Is there anything you feel he would like to change?

FIND THE NOUN

Remember, the way a word is used will determine if it is a noun. Look back over the passage and consider the way each of the following words is used. If it is used as the name of a **person, place, object** or **quality,** then it is a noun.

11   Pick out the nouns!

which	wave	remember	Australia
surprisingly	enough	storm	Brad Mayes
right	of	sea	timed
lull	crazy	area	huge
paddle	was	top	punt
BOOM	loud	along	boards
slide	left	northern	try
inviting	truth	had	up
moment	contact	again	

12   In the article, each of the following words is *not* used as a noun. Make up a sentence using each word as a noun.
(a)   can   (b)   surf   (c)   right   (d)   set
(e)   safe   (f)   flat   (g)   thought   (h)   giant
(i)   bounce   (j)   try

13 Divide the following group of twelve nouns from the passage into two columns, singular and plural.

seas	waves	point	fear
ages	attention	friends	rocks
feet	top	situation	number

Kinds of nouns

Just as there are different kinds of boards (from pin-tails and twin fins to logs and spoons), so there are different kinds of nouns.

The word 'noun' is a bit like a large, handy carry-bag, containing all the name-words used in speech and writing. But there are some differences amongst these name-words. Usually four different kinds of noun are identified: **proper, common, collective,** and **abstract.**

- **Proper** nouns name a particular person or place. They can be identified easily because they always start with a capital letter.

    Bruce Raymond   Bondi
- **Common** nouns are nouns which name classes or kinds of objects, people or places.

    wave   rock   storm   surfer
- **Collective** nouns are used to name groups of things.

    a *bunch* of kids   a *pile* of surfboards
- **Abstract** nouns are used to name qualities, emotions and actions. An abstract noun never has any physical 'body'. It can't be weighed, or put in a test-tube, or touched. It is an abstract thing — not made of physical matter.

    warmth   excitement

What kind of noun is . . . ?

14 (a) Most of the following nouns are from the passage. Draw up four columns in your workbook (Proper, Common, Collective and Abstract) and sort the nouns into their various kinds.

Waimea Bay	wave	crowd	surfboard
Sydney	lull	mob	truth
decision	water	sand	thrill
friends	set (of waves)	pack (of sharks)	

 (b) Add three nouns of your own choice to each column.

Collective nouns

15 Match the correct collective noun from the group on the right, with the group of things it describes.

THING BEING DESCRIBED	COLLECTIVE NOUN
(a) a [.....] of ants	album
(b) a [.....] of roses	school
(c) a [....] of fish	collection
(d) an [.....] of photos	library
(e) a [.....] of records	den
(f) a [.....] of books	bevy
(g) a [.....] of bees	orchestra
(h) a [.....] of birds	host
(i) a [.....] of geese	chain
(j) an [.....] of instruments	haul
(k) a [.....] of ships	bundle
(l) a [.....] of angels	herd
(m) a [.....] of food stores	bunch
(n) a [.....] of old magazines	gaggle
(o) a [.....] of mullet	swarm
(p) a [.....] of thieves	column
(q) a [.....] of elephants	flotilla

Abstract nouns

16 Use each of the words given below as the basis for an abstract noun. It would be a tragedy not to guess the first one.

(a) tragic	(b) bankrupt	(c) manage
(d) inflate	(e) occupy	(f) organise
(g) stable	(h) permit	(i) real
(j) dense	(k) habitable	(l) machine
(m) rotate	(n) monarch	(o) simple

More unusual plurals

Form plurals for the following nouns.

17

(a) lady	(b) valley	(c) story	(d) storey
(e) lily	(f) monkey	(g) dairy	(h) pony
(i) honey	(j) study	(k) entry	(l) jury
(m) property	(n) soliloquy	(o) factory	

18

(a) radio	(b) domino	(c) tornado	(d) biro
(e) lasso	(f) cameo	(g) tomato	(h) tobacco
(i) silo	(j) solo	(k) torso	(l) ratio
(m) quarto	(n) Eskimo		

SYNONYMS AND ANTONYMS

A **synonym** is a word which has a similar meaning to another word. 'Fast' is a synonym for 'quick'. An **antonym** is a word which has the opposite meaning to another word. 'Fast' is an antonym for 'slow'.

19 Find synonyms of your own for the following words.

(a) peaceful	(b) ocean	(c) huge
(d) village	(e) pupil	(f) car
(g) torment	(h) cemetery	(i) healthy
(j) ghost		

20 Choose the **synonym** from the four possibilities for each word.

WORD	POSSIBLE SYNONYM
(a) concise	loud, brief, clever, stylish
(b) custom	tradition, option, dream, buyer
(c) grime	beast, wrong-doing, dirt, rust
(d) withstand	honour, resist, rival, appeal

(e)	contend	swindle, kidnap, struggle, restore
(f)	emotion	sharpness, calm, fashion, feeling
(g)	captivate	consider, kiss, irritate, fascinate
(h)	grateful	thankful, forgotten, flattering, vicious
(i)	grave	serious, ideal, unlucky, deadly
(j)	remedy	danger, cure, tremble, alarm

21 Match the words with their antonyms.

	WORD	ANTONYM
(a)	refreshed	co-operate
(b)	assist	danger
(c)	oppose	defend
(d)	safety	exhausted
(e)	attack	prevent
(f)	permitted	success
(g)	poverty	wisdom
(h)	foolishness	cowardly
(i)	failure	banned
(j)	brave	wealth

22 Form **antonyms** for the following words by adding an extra syllable in front of each word. For example, 'limited' becomes 'unlimited'.

(a) contented	(b) measurable	(c) courteous
(d) connect	(e) literate	(f) complicated
(g) orderly	(h) successful	(i) broken
(j) definite		

PUNCTUATION

Besides the full stop, question marks and exclamation marks may be used at the end of sentences. Note that the title of the extract is an exclamation.

- A full stop (.) ends a statement.
- A question mark (?) ends a question.
- An exclamation mark (!) ends an exclamation.

23 Punctuate the following sentences correctly.
  (a) surfing is an incredible experience
  (b) why are so many young people turned on by surfing
  (c) a lot of kids are keen on surfing these days
  (d) the power of a three metre wave is unbelievable
  (e) how long does it take to become a skilled surfer
  (f) just to hear the surf pumping really makes you feel stoked
  (g) how long will it be before the craze starts to fade
  (h) the correct choice of a surfboard is very important

CHANGE-A-WORD

24   By shuffling the order of the letters in each of the following words,
     you can make a new word. Use the clues to help you. The first
     one is done to give you the idea.

    (a) CHEAT becomes to instruct.   TEACH

    (b) MARCH becomes a magic spell.   [.....]

    (c) DANGER becomes a male goose.   [.....]

    (d) HOSES becomes an item of dress.   [.....]

    (e) MELON becomes a sour fruit.   [.....]

    (f) OVER becomes to wander.   [.....]

    (g) TRACER becomes a part of a volcano.   [.....]

    (h) READ becomes a challenge.   [.....]

    (i) MOPE becomes a piece of literature.   [.....]

    (j) STATE becomes one of the five senses.   [.....]

    (k) HEAPS becomes an outline.   [.....]

    (l) TIMES becomes an old-fashioned hit.   [.....]

THE WRITE APPROACH

Surfing the big ones is an emotional combination of tremendous excitement and fear. Excitement and fear . . . combine these two emotions in your composition, beginning with one of the following sentences.

25 I remember when I first became interested in parachute jumping . . .

26 Skiing isn't for people whose nerves are bad . . .

27 Sailing on the open sea in a small craft has its moments . . .

TALK TIME

28 Use the following letter, reprinted from *Backdoor*, as stimulus material for class discussion.

- Selfishness on our beaches.
- Beach pollution — who is responsible?
- The importance of understanding each other, or tolerance.

The Editor,
Backdoor.

Dear Sir,
I wanted to get mad when I read Brian Monroe's 'Central Coasting' (July '76) but then I thought my answer would turn out as negative as the article itself. So here are some of my thoughts on 'localism', 'hassling', etc.

I'm one of the panel vaned invaders that Brian talks about. (Just forget the 'pimples' and 'moron' bit.) Why the panel van, etc? It's all image. I like the image it all creates in the city. O.K.? 'Locals' don't need an image, but for people who are still in the rat-race an image is unavoidable. Every one in a city is something; if you're not a surfie you're a rocker, or a trendie, or a dope freak, or an intellectual or a worker or a something else.

I may be different from the usual 'crews', but when I'm 'down the coast' everything is changed. I know I'm out classed when I'm in the water, but I don't think I should feel guilty about intruding. After all, can any one person own the ocean?

When I surf I try and surf alone. Usually I find myself in all the shorebreaks and general slop, but I feel that the better surfers can make the good waves far more like a piece of art than I ever could, so I leave them to it. Sometimes, however, I get involved in hassles, and it is sad to see a really good surfer lowering his art by abusing me.

I am waiting for one day when a surfer will say: 'Paddle out with me and I will show you where to wait and which wave to catch'; instead of, 'Drop-in again and I'll smash your face in!' Will I have to wait forever? I hope not.

Surfing in Australia is changing, no longer is it the sport of few; it is becoming the recreation of many, and the very best surfers themselves are making this so. Townend, Farrelly, Rabbit, Lynch, Young and Richards are all out to sell boards, shorts or whatever to the new breed of surfer (and they exist by the thousands).

I respect the sea, the shoreline and the beauty of nature itself very much, and to see empty beer cans and chip packets thrown by 'townie crews' upon that which I love depresses me as well. But can the Brian Monroe's of this world be so pious in their comment, when their own type express their feelings by writing in five-foot high letters on the Adelaide-Victor Harbor Road: 'P... off Townies'. (I just hope the 'locals' who did this were not insulting nature by marvelling at the beauty of the sunset at the time.)

It would be good to live on a nice beach all the time but some of us are too caught up in a society from which we can't escape. Don't deprive us of our short, temporary escapes from hell.

I don't know if I speak for all 'surfies', but I know that I deeply respect true 'surfers'. So please, put up with me at weekends and teach me your art — don't just abuse my lack of it.

Love,
Damian Hull,
Parkside, S.A.

Unit Three: Bomber

This is an extract from the book by Wilhelm Johnen, a German night fighter pilot in the Second World War.

Duel under the stars

Risop suddenly called out: 'There's one above us!'

I could only vaguely recognize the outlines of an enemy aircraft. What a miracle! We had spotted him without a searchlight, without radar and without direction. The bomber was flying at a fairly high speed on a northerly course. My nerves were on edge. I forced myself to be calm and pulled up my nose. Slowly the monster drew closer — to forty, thirty, twenty metres. We must have looked very small and insignificant compared with this mighty 'barn door' with its gigantic wings covering the sky.

'It's a four-engine,' stammered Risop. 'We haven't seen this type before.'

I was now flying close below the bomber and took a breather. The enemy machine continued north-west on its homeward course, presumably quite unaware of the pursuer below. But I made a great mistake. The Tommy had long since spotted me. This was the first time that the Short Stirling four-engined bomber, carrying a ten-tonne load, had appeared in the Ruhr zone. Our defence knew nothing of this type. Risop and I were therefore un-aware that beneath the fuselage sat a gunner with two heavy machine-guns to protect this weak spot.

In blissful ignorance we continued to fly below him, watching the glowing exhaust pipes of the four radial engines.

'How shall we attack?' asked Risop.

I thought for a second and decided that the best method would be from below in order to let the bomber pass across my sights and then to give him a good burst in the fuselage. The most dangerous moment would be when I zoomed behind his tail and the propeller slipstream of his engines caught my aircraft. I there-fore had to aim vertically at his fuselage in order to put 'Tail-end Charlie' out of action.

'It's time to fire,' said Risop. 'Otherwise he'll spot us. Put your trust in God and wade in, *Herr Leutnant*.' Those were his last words.

I throttled back, let the bomber forge ahead and put on top rudder. The protruding nose appeared in my sights. At the same moment our bursts crossed. As out of a watering can, the enemy's tracers bore down on me from all the guns, completely blinding me. My aircraft was caught in the slip-stream and tossed about like a scrap of paper. It was impossible to aim. The broadside of my Me. 110 afforded the Stirling gunner an excellent target and the bullets lashed my cockpit, fuselage and petrol tanks. In a frac-

tion of a second my machine was transformed into a flaming torch.
Scores of litres of petrol were alight, the flames were already licking the cockpit. A machine-gun salvo grazed my left leg and tore
away the bundle of recognition flares attached to my left calf. The
cockpit roof was torn off by the weight of the explosion and flew
away. At this moment of almost certain death, I cast a glance at
Risop. He had slumped forward, lifeless, over his radio. The
machine-gun bursts had killed him. My hope of getting out of the
burning machine as it fell vertically into the yawning depths was
very slight. The appalling heat in this sea of flames almost made
me lose consciousness.

I felt no fear. With a desperate effort, I hoisted my wounded
leg out of the cockpit, but centrifugal force was too strong and
forced me back into the aircraft. So I abandoned all hope of being
saved and put my hands up to shield my eyes. After a dive of 3000
metres the aircraft exploded in the air and flung me out. As a burning torch I hurtled through the air on my back. The cool night
air lashed my face and revived me. Like a flash the thought ran
through my head: the parachute is on fire. The silk cords were
still in the pack protected from the greedy flames. I quickly put
out the flames with both hands and tore off my flying boots and
gloves. I got away with it. It was high time to open the parachute
for the red fires below seemed to be approaching at a terrifying
speed. The earth drew closer and closer. A sudden jerk stopped

my breathtaking fall. The parachute opened. My joy was indescribable but it was soon to be dampened: the parachute was torn and had bullet holes in it. My nerves were at breaking point. And yet somehow I pulled myself together. I was now terribly afraid. During the dive I had hardly had time to realize things for they went too fast. But now in this leisurely descent I saw myself lying at any moment with broken limbs on some street pavement. And yet the earth did not seem to draw any nearer. One of the sixteen lines was shot through and was fluttering in the wind. The parachute was on a slant in the air and threatened at any minute to roman candle. That would have been the end. With my last strength I tugged on the opposite lift webs and righted the canopy. During this last desperate action I crashed heavily into the water of a flooded meadow and sank up to the neck in the mud. Again my luck held. The bad effects of my clumsy landing were offset by the soft soil. The cold water completely revived me. I fired my revolver into the air for someone to come and rescue me. Some men hurried up and freed me from my tricky situation. Then I fainted. When, after some hours, I opened my eyes a sister was bending over me with a smile. I was saved.

WILHELM JOHNEN, *Duel Under the Stars*

Report on the Action between a German Night Fighter and an Enemy Bomber

This report is divided into four sections:

- the **action** between night fighter and bomber
- the **destruction** of the night fighter
- the **escape** of the pilot by parachute
- the parachute **landing**

Answer the questions in your workbook. Keep checking back with the passage all the time. Right, off you go then, and happy landing!

1 The action

(a) How many engines? What kind?

(b) What kind of plane is this?

(d) Bomb weight?

(c) In what area of Germany are they flying?

(e) There is a hidden danger. Where is it? What is it? What nickname is it given?

(f) The pilot and observer spot an enemy aircraft. What a miracle! Give 3 reasons why it's a miracle.

(g) Had they ever seen this type of plane before?

(h) How do they think they must have looked compared with the monstrous enemy plane?

(j) What are the last words the observer ever speaks? (Give his exact words.)

(i) The pilot decides that the best method of attack would be [.....]. Reason? He also decides to aim [.....]. Reason?

(k) What is this plane called?

2   The destruction

(a)   What household object does the author compare the enemy's tracer fire to?

(b)   As the aircraft is tossed about it is compared to [.   .   .   .   .].

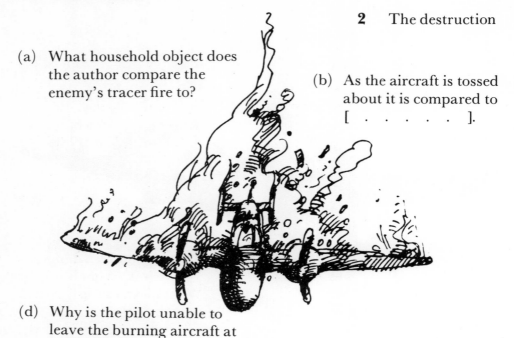

(d)   Why is the pilot unable to leave the burning aircraft at the first try?

(e)   How does the pilot finally manage to leave the burning aircraft?

(c)   The word used for bullets hitting the cockpit, etc., is [.   .   .   .   .].

(g)   What does he compare himself to as he hurtles through the air on his back?

(h)   He is revived by?

(i)   What thought flashes through his mind as he falls?

(j)   'The red fires below seemed to be approaching at a terrifying speed.' What do you think the red fires might have been?

(f)   The plane falls vertically into [.   .   .   .   .]. What?

3 The escape

(a) 'A sudden [.....] stopped my [.....] fall.'

(b) Two strong feelings quickly follow the opening of the parachute. What are these emotions?

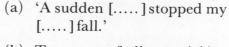

(c) This is called the [.....].

(f) Some of these ropes are called [.....].

(d) The chute is damaged in two places. What is the damage?

(e) Something's wrong with the chute. What?

(a) He comes in for a soft landing. How come?

4 The landing

(c) Who rescues him?

(b) How does he attract attention?

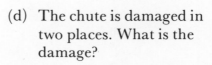

(d) 'Then I fainted [...] smile.' What happens in between?

SPELLING

5   An asterisk (*) indicates words you may not know the meaning of. Look these up in the back-of-the-book dictionary, and write down the words and their meanings side by side in your workbook. If there happens to be more than one meaning for a word, write down the meaning it has in *Duel Under the Stars*.

	vaguely	desperate
	recognize	shield
*	insignificant	parachute
* *	quite	realize
* *	quiet	leisurely
	defence	descent
*	fuselage	canopy
*	blissful	* offset
	propeller	
*	slipstream	
*	protruding	
*	transformed	
*	salvo	
	consciousness	
*	appalling	
	completely	
*	situation	

** 'quite' and 'quiet'
Beware of hang ups about these two little words.
They do have *quite* different meanings.
When you get a *quiet* moment, look them up and put down their different meanings very carefully.

"Next!"

ADJECTIVES COLOUR OUR WORLD

Surf, horses, TV, faces, feet, crowds, pets, garages, supermarkets, pop stars, posters, lawnmowers, dollars, cents —

things   Things   THINGS!

and, of course,

words   Words   WORDS!

Every*thing* is called by at least one word. All these words that refer to things are **nouns.** But nouns couldn't make much of an impact by themselves. They need **adjectives** to give colour, shape, size, strength, feeling or whatever else might be needed to the world of nouns. That's why we can say that 'adjectives colour our world'.

Or, we can put it like this:

Adjectives are

●   words that are always linked with nouns (and pronouns),

●   words that can give a lot more meaning to nouns (and pronouns).

Let's take each function in turn.

Adjectives are always linked . . .

6   Below, there's quite a constellation of words that are all either adjectives or nouns in *Duel Under The Stars*. Links, however, have been broken and adjectives are floating around without nouns, and vice versa.

    ●   Write down the nouns.

    ●   Find the adjectives that you can add sensibly to the nouns, using the spaces to help you decide on single adjectives or groups of adjectives.

    ●   When you've finished, check back with the first six paragraphs of the passage to find out how you went.

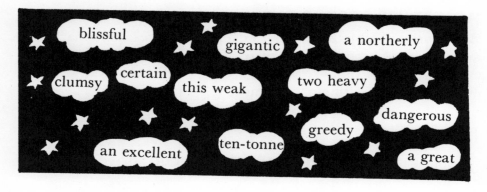

(a) [. . . . .] flames   (b) [. . . . .] death
(c) [. . . . .] mistake   (d) [. . . . .] moment
(e) [. . . . .] course   (f) [. . . . .] ignorance
(g) [. . . . .] wings   (h) [. . . . .] landing
(i) [. . . . .] load   (j) [. . . . .] spot
(k) [. . . . .] target   (l) [. . . . .] machine-guns

Adjectives can give a lot more meaning . . .

Here is a very brief description from *Toilers of the Sea* by Victor Hugo, who shows he knows how to use adjectives to create effect. The following scene shows a man caught by the tentacle of a huge octopus. Notice the adjectives in heavy print.

Suddenly he felt himself seized by the arm. A **strange indescribable** horror thrilled through him.

Some **living** thing, **thin, rough, flat, cold, slimy,** had twisted itself around his **naked** arm, in the **dark** depth below. It crept upward towards his chest. Its pressure was like a **tightening** cord, its **steady** persistence like that of a screw. In less than a moment **some mysterious spiral** form had passed round his wrist and elbow, and had reached his shoulder. A **sharp** point penetrated beneath the armpit.

Here are some kinds of adjectives that you should know —

Adjectives tell **what kind of** — gigantic, dangerous, clumsy, etc.

Adjectives tell **how many** — forty, thirty, ten, two, no, a, an, etc.

Adjectives **point out** — this, these, that, those, the, etc.

Adjectives tell **how much** — much, some, enough, whole, etc.

7   Find the adjectives

Write down the following sentences from *Duel under the Stars* and underline the adjectives.

(a)   I quickly put out the flames with both hands and tore off my flying boots and gloves.

(b)   A sudden jerk stopped my breathtaking fall.

(c)   But I made a great mistake.

(d)   My nerves were at breaking point.

(e)   With my last strength I tugged on the opposite lift webs and righted the canopy.

(f)   The bad effects of my clumsy landing were offset by the soft soil.

(g)   The cold water completely revived me.

(h)   Some men hurried up and freed me from my tricky situation.

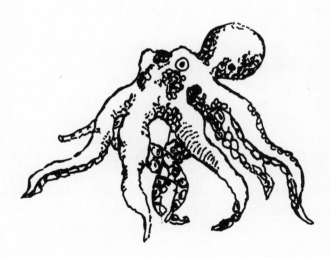

8   Here are some complete sentences from the passage — complete, except for some adjectives that have strayed into the box.

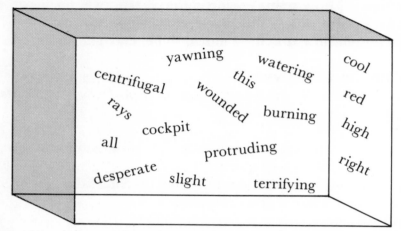

● Rewrite the sentences putting back the right adjectives in the right places.

● When you've finished, check your efforts by finding the complete sentences in the passage.

(a)   With a [.....] effort, I hoisted my [...........] leg out of the cockpit, but [......] force was too strong and forced me back into the aircraft.

(b)   As out of a [.....] can, the enemy's tracers bore down on me from [...] the guns completely blinding me.

(c)   The [.....] nose appeared in my sights.

(d)   The [.....] roof was torn off by the weight of the explosion and flew away.

(e)   The [.....] [........] air lashed my face and revived me.

(f)   My hope of getting out of the [.....] machine as it fell vertically into the [.....] depths was very [.....].

(g)   It was [.....] time to open the parachute for the [.....] fires below seemed to be approaching at a [.....] speed.

(h)   'It's a four-engine,' stammered Risop. 'We haven't seen [.......] type before.'

PUNCTUATION PAUSE — THE COMMA

Commas are most commonly used for the following purposes.

● **Where additional information is given**

> 'This was the first time that the Short Stirling four-engined bomber, **carrying a ten-tonne load**, had appeared in the Ruhr zone.'
>
> 'Risop, **the observer,** was the first to spot the enemy plane.'
>
> 'The pilot, **who was an experienced fighter pilot,** worked out a plan of attack.'

Notice how the words in bold black type give us a little extra information? Also, when reading this sentence out aloud, you would pause briefly, put in the 'carrying a ten-tonne load', pause again, and go on with the main part of the sentence. Try it.

● **Where there are several words that are the same part of speech**

> 'Slowly the monster drew closer — to **forty, thirty, twenty** metres.'
>
> It was painted a **dull, green, non-reflective** colour.
>
> His face was **bearded, lined** and **pale.**

Here the adjectives are broken up into more comfortable pieces of speech by the commas. Read it aloud and you'll find you are grateful for the pauses.

● **Where a person is being spoken to**

> 'Put your trust in God and wade in, **Herr Leutnant**.'
>
> **Risop,** keep your eye on him!
>
> Keep your eye on him, **Risop**!

The comma comes just before the person addressed. It's almost a pause for respect.

9 Put the commas back into the following sentences.

(a) He had slumped forward lifeless over his radio.

(b) When after some hours I opened my eyes a sister was bending over me with a smile.

(c) Fish you are going to have to die anyway.

(d) But I must get him close close close he thought.

(e)   The child you once weaned coddled and pampered is no more.

(f)   He will probably be very hairy have skin blemishes and dress like a hobo.

(g)   However if a tantrum persists I recommend a good pacifier.

(h)   His wife will be dividing her affection between two people: a big self-sufficient figure and a small helpless creature.

(i)   'Just for that you can't play pinochle next Tuesday Junior!'

(j)   They are the right colours . . . red toe blue body suede leather Oxfords.

PUNCTUATION POINT

We must have looked very small and insignificant compared with this mighty barn door with **its** gigantic wings covering the sky.

'**It's** a four-engine,' stammered Risop. 'We haven't seen this type before.'

The only difference between the two words in bold black type is an apostrophe (a kind of high rise comma). The apostrophe shows that two words ('it' and 'is') have been run together and shortened to 'it's'.

Rule: whenever two words have been run together and shortened by dropping a letter, an apostrophe is used right at the spot where the letter used to be.

'**Its**' as in 'its gigantic wings' is used to show possession, and has no apostrophe. Confusing? Yes, because nouns (though *not* pronouns) show possession by adding an 's or s'.

plane's wings (singular)

planes' wings (plural)

But!   its wings (singular)

10   Punctuate the following, putting in the apostrophe where necessary.

(a)   Its time for its food.

(b)   Its mine. Its certainly not yours.

(c)   If its OK with you, I'll give it its last coat of paint.

(d)   Its a problem but its not going to be solved by worrying about it.

(e)   Take it away, its all yours.

MAKE YOUR KNOWLEDGE OF ADJECTIVES WORK!

11 Write an exciting description of a hang glider's flight from go to woe. Make it about a page in length. Here's a plan you might like to use:

TAKE OFF	the successful run and take off from a hill or headland
IN FLIGHT	gliding, soaring without a care in the world till —
FOG!	trapped, and the glider develops a fault
DOWN	faster, much faster than intended
OBSTACLES	looming trees
THE LANDING	It's soft! In whatever you choose, water or mud up to the neck, a haystack, a tyre dump. You choose! Got the idea? OK, then. Good Luck!

TALK TIME

12 Debate topic: That wars are sometimes necessary.

Now let yourself go and zoom in on the square of letters.

13 Here are 20 words that are adjectives describing nouns in the passage:

northerly	gigantic	Ruhr	heavy
weak	dangerous	propeller	protruding
excellent	flaming	machine-gun	yawning
appalling	greedy	red	breathtaking
indescribable	sudden	breaking	sixteen

- Find and list the nouns each adjective describes.
- The nouns are camouflaged in the square of letters. Copy the square of letters into your workbook. Search for the nouns and destroy them by ruling them out!

```
A  M  A  C  H  I  N  E  G  U  N  S
P  O  E  N  T  C  N  L  D  S  A  L
S  H  O  N  J  O  Y  I  E  P  S  I
S  L  I  Z  Z  V  O  N  P  O  L  P
C  O  U  R  S  E  D  E  P  T  H  S
P  F  L  A  M  E  S  S  H  E  A  T
O  S  I  S  Z  O  J  F  L  M  E  R
I  A  F  R  H  F  M  E  D  G  H  E
N  L  A  C  E  L  F  E  R  O  Y  A
T  V  R  J  E  S  Z  A  N  K  T  M
N  O  S  E  O  I  T  H  L  T  H  C
T  A  R  G  W  I  N  G  S  L  S  K
```

Unit Four: Shark

A shark tried to eat me

The attack took place on the 12th March about 2.30 p.m. on Aldinga Reef some forty-eight kilometres south of Adelaide.

I was over half a kilometre from the nearest point of land.

Suddenly I was startled to see two thirty-kilogram yellowtail kingfish swim below me in about eight metres of water. I dived and shot a spear after the fast disappearing large fish.

At this moment it flicked through my mind that after many years diving in South Australian waters, at long last I had seen my first kingfish. I thought, 'Maybe from now on, the recent uneventful chain of events which I have been experiencing may change, and I may even see a large shark today'. To that day I had sighted many sharks, but none had been over three metres in length.

While just preparing for a dive, lying relaxed on the surface, my body was suddenly thrown into a convulsive shudder as I felt my left leg being nearly wrenched from me. I swung around with a stifled scream to witness the nightmarish sight of a four-metre white pointer shark hanging on to it. All panic was gone in an instant as the thought 'You're going to have to be good to get out of this' thudded into my brain.

I remembered reading once about thumbing a shark's eye can make it let go, so I threw my left arm out to try this, only to find the shark had let my leg go and my outstretched hand went down its throat. I dragged it back in desperation, little knowing how close I must have been to losing it.

The white pointer then went into a fast, tight circle and came charging straight back. It was not without a sense of malicious glee that I swung the gun around and dived to meet the onslaught. Obviously it was now or never. The spear thudded into its massive head about seven centimetres behind the left eye. The impact appeared to stop the shark and it shook its body, trying to free itself of the one and a half metre stainless steel spear. This it soon did. During the fury of the moment I will never forget the actual thrill of spearing such a monster. It may sound a little absurd, but that is how the mind seems to work at times under moments of extreme stress.

A great tail disappearing into the blue was the last I saw of my attacker, heading in a southerly direction.

BRIAN RODGER

Check your understanding
1 Where was Brian Rodger when he was attacked?
2 What startled him?
3 Had there been much excitement in his spear fishing recently?
4 What did he hope to see?
5 How did the shark first reveal itself to him?
6 What did he do, feel, see, and think as he swung around?

SHARK 43

7 He threw his left arm out towards the shark. What was he trying to do? What happened?
8 What did he feel as he dived to meet the shark's onslaught?
9 Brian Rodger says that there is something he will never forget. What is it?
10 What does he say about his last sight of the shark?

Pinpointing meanings

11 Some of the words and phrases used by Brian Rodger in describing how he was attacked by the white pointer may be unfamiliar. Pinpoint their meanings in the following exercise.

• Choose the correct meaning from the brackets. To help you choose the correct meaning, find the word in the passage. Take each of the bracketed meanings in turn, and test it to see which one fits best.

• Complete the sentence. The first one has been completed for you as an example.

(a) What does 'uneventful' mean?
   (a) that nothing goes wrong
   (b) that nothing exciting happens
   (c) that it is fine and sunny
   'Uneventful' means that nothing exciting happens.

(b)   What is 'experiencing'?
   (a)   something you really want to happen
   (b)   living, feeling and undergoing things
   (c)   anything you can do without
'Experiencing' is . . .

(c)   What is a 'convulsive shudder'?
   (a)   a sudden, violent shake or tremble
   (b)   a quick, darting movement ending in a grab
A convulsive shudder is . . .

(d)   When something is 'wrenched' it is?
   (a)   pulled violently
   (b)   twisted firmly
   (c)   treated badly
'Wrenched' is when something is . . .

(e)   What is a scream that is 'stifled'?
   (a)   turned into a bellow
   (b)   carefully controlled
   (c)   choked
A stifled scream is a scream that is . . .

(f)   What does 'witness' mean?
   (a)   seeing something
   (b)   finding something
'Witness' means . . .

(g)   What does 'in desperation' mean?
   (a)   without any kind of feeling
   (b)   in a reckless and almost hopeless way
'In desperation' means . . .

(h)   How would you show 'malicious glee'?
   (a)   by wishing somebody evil
   (b)   by getting spiteful pleasure out of something
You would show 'malicious glee' . . .

(i)   What does 'onslaught' mean?
   (a)   a slow, circling approach
   (b)   a violent attack
'Onslaught' means . . .

(j) When something is 'massive' it is?
    (a) short and squat
    (b) huge and heavy
    (c) silent and deadly
    Something is 'massive' when it is . . .

(k) What does 'absurd' mean?
    (a) silly and funny
    (b) weird and strange
    (c) difficult and serious
    'Absurd' means . . .

(l) Something (or someone) is under 'extreme stress' when it is?
    (a) under a kind of long-lasting spell
    (b) under very great strain
    (c) undergoing great change
    When something or someone is under 'extreme stress' it is...

NOUNS AND ADJECTIVES

12 Look back through the passage and see if you can supply the adjectives that link up with the nouns listed below. Note that the first letter of the word is given, as well as the number of letters in the word. (The first one has been completed as an example.)

	ADJECTIVES	NOUNS
(a)	nearest	point of land
(b)	m . . .	years
(c)	f	kingfish
(d)	l	shark
(e)	m . . .	sharks
(f)	c	shudder
(g)	s	scream
(h)	n	sight
(i)	l . . .	arm
(j)	o	hand
(k)	m	glee
(l)	m	head

USING ADJECTIVES

13 Draw an outline of a shark. On your drawing, indicate with arrows the following things:

jaws   teeth   body   fins   eyes   tail

Leave space *in front of* each of the nouns for an adjective or adjectives.

....tail

14 Give your nouns the adjective(s) that seem to fit them best from the following list:

cold	massive	triangular	powerful
razor-sharp	staring	great	streamlined
gaping	sickle-shaped		

Variety

As well as putting adjectives *in front of* the nouns they refer to, it is often possible to create variety and interest by putting them

- *before* and *after* the nouns they refer to,
- *after* the nouns they refer to.

All adjectives **in front of** the noun	Some adjectives **in front,** some **after** the noun	All adjectives **after** the noun
The *silent, ruthless* killer	The *silent* killer is* *ruthless*.	The killer is* *silent* and* *ruthless*.

*Notice how 'is' and 'and' are added.

15 Draw up 3 columns as above. Switch adjectives around in the following sentences by using 'is' and 'and'.

(a) The tough, fearless swimmer
(b) The sudden ferocious attack
(c) The calm, blue, unruffled surface of the sea
(d) The long, heavy, torpedo-like body
(e) The strange, dim, underwater world

SPELLING

16 Complete the spelling of the words with the missing letters by getting your neighbour to find the words in the passage and read them out to you. Check with the passage to find your score out of 14.

(a) the fast [disap . . . . ing] large fish.
(b) I dragged it back in [desper . . . . n].
(c) I have been [exper . . . . ing].
(d) [mal . . . ous] glee.
(e) [obv . . . . ly] it was now or never.
(f) moments of [ext . . . e] stress.
(g) it may sound a little [ab . . . d].
(h) with a [st . . . . d] scream.
(i) [sud . . . . y] I was startled.
(j) I will never forget the [act . . .] thrill.
(k) to [wit . . . .] the nightmarish sight.
(l) the [i . . . . t] appeared to stop the shark.
(m) the last I saw of my [at . . . . er].
(n) dived to meet the [on . . . . . ht].

BEGINNING AND ENDING SENTENCES

Normally speaking, all sentences **begin** with a capital letter.
Sentences can be **ended** with a full stop, a question mark, or an exclamation mark   .   ?   !

stating a fact   **asking a question**   **exclaiming**

The spear-gun is loaded.   Don't point that thing at me!

Did you say you'd loaded it?

capital letter   capital letter   capital letter
          full stop   question mark   exclamation mark

17   Use all 3 kinds of sentence endings in your own version of 'A Shark Tried to Eat Me'. Follow the composition plan given below, in which you are guided by paragraph headings and lead sentences.

(a)   *A Monster Shark Is Sighted.*
        The surfies lounging under the red umbrella leapt to their feet and began pointing out to sea. I . . .

(b)   *As a Trained Shark Hunter You Decide to Investigate.*
        Not wanting to waste a second, I began checking my underwater gear as the coastguards rushed me to the spot. Once there . . .

(c)   *There's No Sign of the Shark — At First.*
        The sea looked clear — in every direction except one . . .

(d)   *The Attack!*
        My left flipper was ripped off . . .

(e)   *The Shark is Beaten Off.*
        It had been a terrible battle for survival . . .

(f)   *The Crowd on the Beach Goes Wild.*
        Back on the beach I was given a great welcome back from the jaws of death. I . . .

FISHING FOR ADJECTIVES ABOUT THE SHARK

In the following nets of words, look at the clues, and fill in the answers downwards.

When you've successfully completed this, you'll find that one of the *across* words is an adjective used in the passage to describe either the shark or something about the shark.

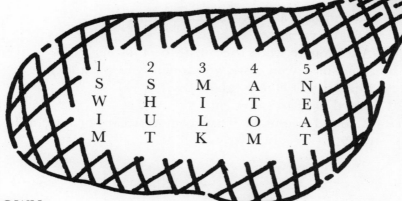

```
1     2     3     4     5
S     S     M     A     N
W     H     I     T     E
I     U     L     O     A
M     T     K     M     T
```

DOWN

1 Something humans can do but sharks can do better.
2 Not open.
3 Good with cereal in the morning.
4 .... bomb.
5 Another adjective meaning 'tidy'.

18 Draw a rectangle with 7 squares across and 4 squares down. Here are the clues for words downwards that will give you, when completed, a shark adjective *across* the rectangle.
1 Past tense of 'come'.
2 Not hilly.
3 Abbreviation for 'suitcase'.
4 . . . . . s are red, violets are blue.
5 Sky water.
6 A way of getting into a pool.
7 Plural of 'foot'.

19 Draw a rectangle with 11 squares across and 4 down. Here are the clues that will once again give you a shark adjective *across* the rectangle once the downwards words have been correctly completed.

1 What you feel when you hurt yourself.
2 Adjective used to describe a very short skirt.
3 Worn on the finger.
4 'Low'.
5 Faster than a walk, slower than a gallop.
6 A baby carriage.
7 Affectionate word used instead of 'father'.
8 You smell, you taste, you touch, you see and you . . . ?
9 Opposite of clue 2 (above).
10 Word used to call a cat.
11 A sound you make when you are weary or miserable.

Unit Five: Car

Night of the Mustang

My watch showed 12.40 a.m. on the Pacific Highway outside the deserted playground of the Holy Family Roman Catholic Church School at Lindfield.

The red brick church walls and the faces of several dozen people are lit up in alarmingly psychedelic reds and blues by the rotating beacons of two ambulances and several police cars. In this macabre light we can see contorted wreckage of a royal blue Ford Mustang sports car, worth, someone remarks almost wistfully, more than 10,000 bucks.

Beside the car lie two bodies, and we know at least one of them is alive, although I can't think why. The one near me is bleeding from his face and is ominously quiet. Inside the wreck is another man, trapped in an awful grimace of jagged metal, smashed plastic and bloodied upholstery.

We are gathered here, all of us half anxious to do something, half curious, to watch the death of N.S.W. road victim number 227. Ronald Ian Wildman, 25, who lived at Beaumont Road, Killara. He dies quietly after being tossed around in the car in which he was a passenger.

I was on my way home when I saw the wreck. The car had apparently hit the median strip as it was travelling north and veered across the road into a tree near the church. A jacket of bark is stripped from the tree, the tree's pods are flung a long way up the highway and somehow the car managed to fling itself around the tree in a ghastly maypole dance and end up on the side exactly opposite to the direction from which it had come.

People are staggering, half asleep, out of their houses and all are saying, 'Call an ambulance, someone.' One of the car's occupants is lying on the road and we try to do futile things to comfort him. Someone else says that a guy is still inside and oughtn't we to try to get him out?

We try but it's no good; he looks too bad to be moved in any way. Then the ambulance men pull up and we thankfully move away, feeling utterly useless as we murmur things about 'Let us know if you want a hand, mate.'

They get crowbars to work and the man seems to be groaning, weakly. Oxygen comes out of the ambulance. A petite and pretty young blonde in a trouser suit runs up and says, 'I'm a nurse. Can I help?' Several men are walking around the injured, bleeding bodies and murmuring quietly. One of them, we are told, is the father of one of the men who I think is dying.

More people in pyjamas are gathering around asking what happened, and a woman goes to a wall to be sick. The man beside me murmurs, 'These bloody cars are too powerful . . . too powerful . . .' and goes on repeating it to himself.

The police are here and one young constable shouts, 'Did anyone see it happen?' Several people gather around him and he takes notes while another policeman officiously moves people away from the wreckage.

A journalist with a notebook in his hand picks up the Mustang's rear vision mirror, 15 metres from the car with a whole but fractured windscreen. He puts the mirror in the car as four people lift the man out of the wreckage.

The other man is still lying on the roadway receiving oxygen; another on the other side of the car is lifted into one of the two ambulances. Then all three of the Mustang's occupants are in the ambulances, which do a U-turn over a nearby pedestrian crossing and hurtle off down the highway.

ROBERT MAYNE, *The Sydney Morning Herald,*
Saturday, March 20th, 1971

Check your understanding

1 File a report in your workbook on the following details of the accident.
   (a) TIME . . .
   (b) ROAD . . .
   (c) NEARBY BUILDING . . .
   (d) SUBURB . . .
   (e) MAKE OF VEHICLE . . .
   (f) COLOUR OF VEHICLE . . .
   (g) VALUE OF VEHICLE . . .
2 How many people were injured?
3 How bad were the injuries?
4 Explain how the accident happened.
5 Why did the crowd which gathered at the scene of the accident feel helpless?
6 What trained person arrived who did offer help?
7 Some of the people gathered around were badly upset by the accident. How did they show this?
8 How could this article help cut down the road toll?
9 Look up the meanings of the following words in the back-of-the-book dictionary. Write down words and meanings side by side in your workbook.
   (a) psychedelic (b) macabre (c) contorted (d) futile
   (e) officiously (f) ominously (g) grimace (h) petite
   (i) wistfully (j) upholstery (k) fractured

VERBS

- Verbs are doing, being, and having words.
- Verbs tell us what is done or is happening.
- Verbs tell us what the noun (or pronoun) which is the subject of a sentence does or is.
- Every sentence must contain at least one verb.
- Verbs are often made up of more than one word.

the car **crashed** into the pole.

'Crashed' tells us what the car did. 'Crashed' is a verb.

The ambulance **is skidding** to a stop.

'Is skidding' tells us what the ambulance is doing. 'Is skidding' is a verb.

Find the verbs

10 Write down these sentences from *Night of the Mustang* and underline the verbs. Remember that some verbs are made up of more than one part. Some sentences have more than one verb.

(a) I was on my way home when I saw the wreck.

(b) The car had apparently hit the median strip as it was travelling north and veered across the road into a tree near the church.

(c) Beside the car lie two bodies, and we know at least one of them is alive.

(d) A jacket of bark is stripped from the tree, the tree's pods are flung a long way up the highway.

(e) Then the ambulance men pull up and we thankfully move away.

(f) Someone else says that a guy is still inside.

(g) Oxygen comes out of the ambulance.

(h) He puts the mirror in the car as four people lift the man out of the wreckage.

(i)   More people in pyjamas are gathering around.
(j)   The police are here.

Verbs tell the time

Verbs indicate the time an action takes place. There are three main time periods — **present, future,** and **past.** The time which a verb indicates is called its **tense.**

Present Tense	
Singular	Plural
I drive	We drive
You drive	You drive
He/she drives	They drive

'I am driving' and 'I do drive,' are other forms of the present tense.

Future Tense	
Singular	Plural
I shall drive	We shall drive
You will drive	You will drive
He/she will drive	They will drive

'I will drive' and 'I shall be driving' are other forms of the future tense.

Past Tense	
Singular	Plural
I drove	We drove
You drove	You drove
He/she drove	They drove

'I was driving' is another form of the past tense. (In the next book, we'll look at 'I have driven,' which is known as the perfect tense.)

11 Fill in the blanks in the tense tables. The first one has been done to help you.

	Present Time	Future Time	Past Time
(a)	He catches	He will catch	He caught
(b)	He knows		
(c)			He said
(d)		He will drive	
(e)	He rises		

12

	Present Time	Future Time	Past Time
(a)	I am choosing	I shall be choosing	I was choosing
(b)	I am leaving		
(c)		I shall be speaking	
(d)			I was writing
(e)	I am seeing		
(f)		I shall be falling	

13

	Present Time	Future Time	Past Time
(a)	They stand	They will stand	They stood
(b)	They swim		
(c)		They will ride	
(d)			They taught
(e)		They will fight	
(f)	They feel		

Present tense

14 In much of *Night of the Mustang*, the journalist Robert Mayne has used the present tense to make his story more dramatic and realistic. We really get the feeling that he was there at the time. We have jotted down a number of sentences that particularly do this. Write them down and underline their verbs. (Make sure that if a verb has two parts you underline both parts.)

(a) People are staggering.

(b) The one near me is bleeding.

(c) One of the car's occupants is lying on the road.

(d) Another policeman officiously moves people away from the wreckage.

15 The following passage has been taken from the book, *Swiss Family Robinson*, which has since been made into a television series. Change the tense of the passage from past to present by altering the verbs in bold black type.

Boa

As the poor animal **arrived** near the lair of the snake, we suddenly **saw** a terrible head raised above the reeds. The donkey **perceived** his danger, but, instead of fleeing from it, **stood** as if fascinated, and **uttered** a low groan. The boa **approached** steadily with hungry jaws opened wide. Still the donkey **held** his ground, and **gazed** at the monster, which the next minute **wound** its long, scaly body round him, and **suffocated** him in the horrible embrace. We **shuddered** as we **looked** on the fearful sight.

SPELLING

All the work in this section is related to these twenty words which have been taken from *Night of the Mustang*.

although	direction	happen	young
quiet	mirror	receive	vision
anxious	police	people	opposite
curious	pedestrian	occupant	manage
passenger	oxygen	several	weakly

16 Write down words that have *opposite* meanings to the following.
   (a) young   (b) receive   (c) quiet
   (d) weakly   (e) anxious

17 Write down the following sentences and insert the correct words from the brackets.
   (a) The student is very [.....] in class. [quite, quiet]
   (b) The student is [.....] a bad speller. [quite, quiet]
   (c) The teacher received his [.....] magazine. [weakly, weekly]
   (d) The teacher staggered [.....] out of the room. [weakly, weekly]

18 Write down the spelling words in alphabetical order.

19 Unscramble the letters to make up words in the spelling list.
   (a) r i r m r o
   (b) a m g w e a
   (c) v i c e r e e
   (d) p a e n p h
   (e) o l p e p e

USING VERBS EFFECTIVELY

Below is a brief extract from the famous novel *The Caine Mutiny*. In this passage the author has made the scene come to life by his use of verbs. Write down the verbs in the passage and their meanings. (You may have to consult the dictionary at the back of the book.)

In a typhoon

A roaring wave broke over the *Caine's* bridge and buffeted the ship far over to port and Captain Queeg tumbled to his hands and knees. The other officers slid and tottered about. Once again the minesweeper laboured in difficulties as the wind caught it and swept it sideways. Mark went to the telegraph stand and manipulated the engines, altering the settings frequently, and shouting swift changing rudder orders. He coaxed the ship around to the south and steamed ahead until the hulk came vaguely in view again. Then he commenced a circling manoeuvre keeping the *Caine* well clear of the foundering wreck.

20 Try this crossword.

ACROSS
1 Without sound.
5 Having sharp projections.
6 Change direction.
7 One who goes on foot.

DOWN
2 Hurt.
3 Walks unsteadily.
4 One who takes or accepts.

THE WRITE APPROACH

21 Write about twenty lines putting forward your attitude to motor bikes.

22 'A motor cyclist is eight times more likely to be killed than a car driver.' (*Traffic Accident Research Unit Report.*) Put forward arguments in favour of banning motor cycles from the road.

23 Write about twenty lines on 'The Car I Should Like To Own'.

24 Describe what happened to this car. Who was the driver? Was the driver injured or killed? What was the cause of this accident — alcohol, carelessness, tiredness, stupidity, a fault in the car itself? Did the story have a happy ending or not? Write twenty lines.

TALK TIME

25 'There are too many young drivers on the road. No one should be allowed to drive a car until he/she is twenty years of age.' How far do you agree with this statement?

26 Organize a discussion on ways to reduce road accidents. You could discuss some of the following: (a) the job of the police, (b) alcohol, (c) speed, (d) the condition of the roads, (e) pedestrian crossings and traffic lights, (f) powerful cars, (g) safety cars, (h) human weaknesses.

Unit Six: Bushranger

Ben Hall — Bushranger

The bushrangers tethered their horses to saplings in front of the hut and entered Toodle's shanty. Darkness fell, the fire on the hearth subsided to embers, and the bushrangers, wrapped in blankets, slept on the floor of the hut, one of them remaining on watch at the door. From custom they slept lightly, taking watches of an hour each in turn. A whispered word and noiselessly the watch was changed as each man's time on guard expired.

Towards dawn, while Johnny Vane was on duty at the door, a patrol of mounted police approached the hut.

'H-s-s-t!' whispered Vane. 'Traps!'

Instantly the other four were awake. Ben Hall took command. 'The place is surrounded,' he said. 'We'll have to shoot our way out. They can see our horses, so they know we're here.'

Four mounted troopers were looking at the horses tethered in front of Toodle's hut, and apparently conferring as to their next move.

'We'll have to shoot,' continued Ben grimly. 'But hold your fire till I give the word. And remember, don't shoot to kill unless you have to. Shoot their horses in the legs and we'll make our getaway before they can collect their wits.'

Tense pause, as the troopers rode nearer.

'Let them have it,' said Ben.

The silence of dawn was shattered by a volley from the five desperadoes inside the shanty. All the police horses were hit. They reared, some bolted. The police fired wildly at the hut.

Darting outside, firing as they ran, the bushrangers reached their own tethered horses and galloped into the bush, unscathed. The battle was all over in a few minutes.

The gang halted in a patch of scrub near Wallendbeen station, several kilometres away. All were excited, laughing at their escape. They dismounted for a breather.

'Anybody hurt?' was Hall's first question.

'I nearly broke my neck,' grinned Vane. 'My saddle girth was loose and it slipped around under my horse's belly. I had to undo the buckle and let the saddle go.'

'It doesn't make much difference to you, Johnny, riding bareback,' chuckled the leader.

'We'll soon get another saddle,' commented O'Meally.

He pointed to the Cootamundra road, visible in the distance. Over the hill came a solitary horseman, a civilian, riding from Cootamundra towards Murrumburrah.

'Blow me if it isn't John Barnes,' continued O'Meally. 'That's the old cow who fired at us when we got some blankets from him a while ago. His bullet just whizzed past my cheek. I owe the old swab one for that.'

'Don't kill him,' said Hall. 'Just stick him up and take his horse, bridle, saddle and all.'

'This is a one-man job,' said O'Meally excitedly. 'Leave it to me. You four wait here and spell your horses. Watch the fun.'

Quickly he mounted and galloped alone to meet the traveller. Mr Barnes, a respectable, middle-aged, prosperous-looking citizen, was nearing Wallendbeen homestead when O'Meally accosted him, revolver in hand.

'Bail up, you old cow!' he commanded.

'I've got no money with me,' protested Barnes.

'Never mind your dirty money. It's your horse I want, or rather your saddle for one of my mates. Your spavined nag isn't worth taking.'

'I know you, Johnny O'Meally,' said Barnes. 'You're a villain and I'll see you hung some day.'

'Will you?' sneered O'Meally. 'If you give me any more lip, I'll put a bullet in your guts. Get down off that mongrel nag of yours, and walk.'

'Damn you!' yelled the storekeeper. He crouched low, dug spurs into his horse's flanks and attempted to ride towards the homestead, only a hundred metres away.

Calmly O'Meally took aim with his revolver and fired. His first shot struck the storekeeper, but did not unhorse him. O'Meally galloped in pursuit, firing again and again, right up to the gates of Wallendbeen.

Barnes fell from the saddle, dead.

Squatter Mackay, the owner of Wallendbeen, came running out to see what was wrong.

'Will you stop now, you old b————?' yelled O'Meally, looking down at the bleeding corpse of Barnes. To Mr Mackay he explained, 'He should have stopped when I told him to stop. He's dead now, by the look of it, and it serves him right. He said he'd see me hung,' continued the murderer hysterically, 'but he'll never see me hung. I've knocked him stiff, no doubt about that!'

Squatter Mackay knelt and examined the corpse. His face was grim.

'You've murdered him,' he said. 'The law will get you for it, Johnny O'Meally. I know you and I've known your old dad for many years. This is the worst thing you've done in your wicked life.'

'No preaching,' yelled O'Meally, 'or you'll get the same as Barnes got.' His face contorted in a black scowl, the murderer spurred away.

FRANK CLUNE, *Ben Hall the Bushranger*

Check your understanding

1   What precautions did the bushrangers take against being surprised in the night by the police?
2   Why did the police suspect that the bushrangers might be in Toodle's shanty?
3   Why did Ben suggest shooting at the police horses' legs?
4   Explain how Vane narrowly escaped being captured by the police.
5   What do you learn about Ben Hall as a person when he says to O'Meally: 'Don't kill him'?
6   Why did O'Meally have a dislike for Barnes even before he tried to get his saddle from him?
7   What comment would you make about O'Meally as a person when the author says: 'Calmly O'Meally took aim with his revolver and fired'?
8   Do you agree with O'Meally when he says: 'It serves him (Barnes) right'?
9   What did O'Meally mean when he said to Squatter Mackay: 'No preaching'?
10 What is the meaning of the following words? (a) unscathed, (b) prosperous, (c) civilian, (d) solitary, (e) tethered, (f) sapling. If you don't know or are unsure, look up the dictionary at the back of this book.

THE VERB 'TO BE'

One of the most used and most important verbs in the English language
is the verb 'to be'. It has eight forms:

am	be	was
is	being	were
are	been	

11 See whether you can put the correct form of the verb 'to be' in
the spaces below. Consult the story if you are unsure.
  (a) A whispered word and noiselessly the watch [.....] changed
       as each man's time on guard expired.
  (b) Towards dawn, while Johnny Vane [.....] on duty at the door,
       a patrol of mounted police approached the hut.
  (c) 'The place [.....] surrounded,' he said. 'We'll have to shoot
       our way out.'
  (d) 'My saddle girth [.....] loose and it slipped around under my
       horse's belly.'
  (e) Squatter Mackay knelt and examined the corpse. His face
       [.....] grim.
  (f) 'This [.....] the worst thing you've done in your wicked
       life.'

CONTRACTIONS AND THEIR APOSTROPHES

In the English language, there are quite a few **contractions.** A contraction is a shortening of one word or two words by taking away letters
or sounds. An apostrophe is inserted in its place.

it's = it is

12 Write down these contractions from the *Ben Hall* extract. Next to
them write out their full form.
  (a) We'll   (b) We're   (c) Don't   (d) Doesn't
  (e) Isn't   (f) I've   (g) I'll   (h) He's
  (i) He'd   (j) You've   (k) It's   (l) You're
  (m) That's

13   Below are sentences from the story that have apostrophes missing. Write down the sentences and insert the apostrophes in the correct positions.
   (a)   'And remember, dont shoot to kill unless you have to.'
   (b)   'Well soon get another saddle,' commented O'Meally.
   (c)   'Blow me if it isnt John Barnes,' continued O'Meally.
   (d)   'Ill put a bullet in your guts.'
   (e)   'Hell never see me hung. Ive knocked him stiff, no doubt about that!'
   (f)   'This is the worst thing youve done in your wicked life.'

WORD ORDER IN SENTENCES

14   Correct word order is important if sentences are to have meaning for the reader. Rearrange the words in the following sentences so that the sentences make sense. Then check the original.
   (a)   were all horses the hit police
   (b)   with and revolver calmly fired aim O'Meally his took
   (c)   grim his was face
   (d)   traveller the meet to alone galloped and mounted he quickly
   (e)   hut wildly police at the fired the

VERBS AGREE WITH THEIR SUBJECTS

When the subject of a verb is singular, the verb too must be singular; when the subject is plural, the verb must be plural in form.

15   Write down the following sentences and insert the correct form of the missing verb from the brackets at the end of each sentence.
   (a)   The bushrangers [.....] Toddle's shanty. [is entering, are entering]
   (b)   Johnny Vane [.....] on duty at the door. [am, is, were]
   (c)   Hold your fire till I [.....] the word. [give, gives]
   (d)   The police [.....] wildly at the hut. [fires, fired]
   (e)   If you [.....] me any more lip I'll put a bullet in your guts. [give, gives]

(f)   His face [.....] grim. [was, were, are]
(g)   Don't shoot to kill unless you [.....] to. [has, have]
(h)   My saddle girth [.....] loose. [was, were]
(i)   All [.....] excited, laughing at their escape. [was, were]
(j)   The battle [.....] all over in a few minutes. [was, were]

MATCH THE VERBS WITH THE NOUNS

16   In the left-hand column there are groups of words which contain nouns. In the other column there are groups of words which contain verbs. Write down the left-hand column and then match each group with the appropriate words from the other column.

(a) The bushrangers	whizzed past
(b) The place	were hit
(c) The battle	examined the corpse
(d) The fire	slept
(e) The bullet	is surrounded
(f) The saddle girth	was over
(g) Squatter Mackay	subsided
(h) The police horses	fired wildly
(i) The police	was loose
(j) The murderer	spurred away

QUOTATION MARKS AND INVERTED COMMAS

When we write the words actually spoken by someone, we enclose them in quotation marks (or inverted commas, as they are also called).

> 'Let them have it,' said Ben.
> 'Will you?' sneered O'Meally.

Did you notice that the first word actually spoken has a capital letter? Notice also the use of the comma just *inside* the closing quotation mark. Notice, however, that a full stop is used when the sentence is reversed.

> Ben said, 'Let them have it.'
> Vane grinned, 'I nearly broke my neck.'

17   The sentences below come from the story, but their punctuation marks have been removed. See whether you can put them back correctly.

(a)   youve murdered him he said

(b)   blow me if it isnt john barnes continued omeally

(c)   this is a one-man job said omeally excitedly

TALK TIME

18   Discuss or debate the following topics.

(a)   Laws are made to be broken.

(b)   Crime does not pay.

(c)   Police should not be allowed to carry firearms.

19   What crimes do you consider serious?

20   Should a drunken driver be sent to gaol?

21   Is shoplifting more serious than avoiding paying for a railway ticket? Why?

22   Do you think big department stores encourage shoplifting by having their goods openly displayed and few shop assistants to supervise them?

23   Is violence on the increase in our community?

24   How should drug offenders be punished? Differentiate between those taking hard and soft drugs. What about beer drinkers and those who smoke?

25   Bring in some newspaper articles on crime and/or punishment and read them out to the class. Put forward your views on them.

26   Is punishment the best way to stop crime?

DISCUSSION AND WRITING

27   Look at the picture.

(a)   What kind of punishment should the bag snatcher receive when he is caught?

(b)   How can this kind of crime be prevented?

(c)   Now try your hand at writing a newspaper report of this robbery. Pretend you are the woman in the picture. Give your impression of the robbery in about a paragraph.

1. *Speed is the best weapon of the purse snatcher.*

2. *He selects the victim...*

3. *Grabs the bag and disappears into the crowd.*

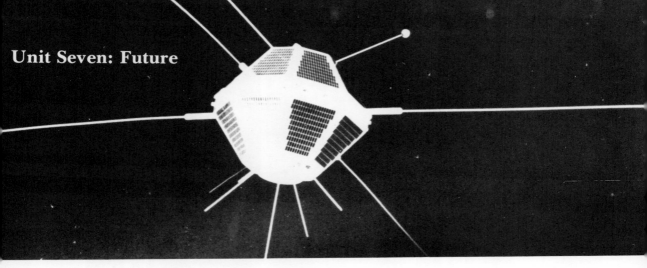

Life will be one long holiday, with plenty of spending money.

For the world's greatest-ever boom is on the way.

The next 10 years should see the biggest economic growth ever.

No one will work more than a three-day week and most dirty jobs will be done by robots.

Towards the end of the century, the boom will level off.

People will have all the consumer goods they can possibly use, and they will resist new developments because they are quite happy as they are.

Art form

They will be able to live as they please, spending their time on things like cooking and painting.

But a major danger is the threat to the earth's atmosphere.

The world in 200 years

Space travel could damage the ozone layer around the earth.

This is the layer of gas which protects us from the harmful effects of the sun.

The amount of space travel at present has no effect.

But in the next century man may abuse space. Ships could leave earth as regularly as planes leave Mascot Airport.

Every time a space ship passes through the ozone layer it damages it.

A depleted ozone layer would allow deadly ultra-violet rays through, possibly causing wide-spread skin cancer.

The sun will provide plenty of energy, and people will learn how to tap the heat at the centre of the earth.

We'll all be healthy

Good health will be guaranteed. Artificial organs — hearts, livers and kidneys — will be perfected.

Everyone will live longer and if anyone develops an illness for which there is no known cure he will be deep-frozen until a cure is found.

There will also be a cure for crime — probably a *Clockwork Orange* type of brain surgery which changes a criminal's personality.

There may be compulsory birth control to prevent people of low intelligence being born.

And parents will be able to choose the sex of their children. Governments will have to decide how to regulate this so that there will not be too many of either sex.

Scientists will be making humans from skin cells within the next 200 years.

Nightmare monsters may be bred. Already in Stanford University School of Medicine in America they have 'created' a creature that is a combination of a toad and a bacterium.

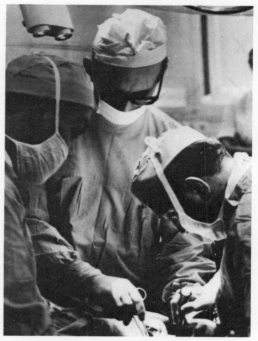

Because this may lead to the creation of incurable disease, research has been stopped.

Work could start again in space labs orbiting the earth.

Food, too

Eating habits will change, too.

Famine is on the way out. Everyone, wherever they live, will eat well.

But the food they eat may be made from things that we throw away.

They will make synthetic foods from unlikely substances such as petrol and cellulose, leaves and ordinary household waste. Crops will be grown on furrows lined with film and fed by liquid manure.

It's a technique already perfected at the Grasshouse Crops Research Institute in Sussex, England.

It is very reliable and already used in 20 countries.

If the Sahara were farmed like this it could feed the world.

Windmills

Flat, windy areas will be dotted with super-efficient windmills that will store power.

They will also harness the power of the waves, and extract heat from the sea in tropical areas.

But the heat of the sun will be the main source of power.

They will be skilled at converting the sun's rays into electricity.

People will need to store all the extra energy from new sources.

Most methods will be improved versions of techniques we use today.

But there will be one very good new method which is now in the pioneer stage — the fly-wheel.

These are wheels that spin so fast that they can contain energy, and release it for conversion into electricity when it is required.

FLOATING CITIES

Parts of the oceans will be covered with floating cities in 200 years time.

We are already experimenting in the Pacific with floating buildings.

Their advantage is that they are not affected by high winds or earthquakes.

Cars will be all-electric and they will be cheaper than cars today.

They will be silent and they won't foul up the air as petrol-burning cars do.

Batteries today don't store enough electricity for electric cars to travel long distances.

But we already have advanced storage batteries that store 10 times as much energy as lead batteries.

Pick your identity

People will buy clothes to suit their hobbies or interests.

Those who belong to a Wild West club will live and dress like cowboys and Indians.

Today, you go to the hairdresser with a picture of a style you like, and ask him to recreate it for you.

In the future, people will be able to pop into their local cosmetic surgeon and ask him to give them a completely new face.

Criminals will change their faces to keep ahead of the police.

And there may be laws banning anyone from 'forging' another person's identity.

Check your understanding

1 Give one reason why life will be one long holiday in 200 years.

2 Why is space travel likely to harm the earth?

3 Where will the main supplies of energy come from?

4 Why will the car of the future be better than today's cars?

5 How will the world's food situation be improved?

6 Why will we have a better chance of living longer in 200 years time?

7 How will criminals be prevented from committing further crimes?

8 What do you think the writer means by his words 'forging another person's identity'?

9 Why aren't electrical cars being successfully used today?

10 What are the meanings of the following words as used in the article?

    (a) boom   (b) synthetic   (c) cosmetic
    (d) depleted   (e) identity   (f) pioneer
    (g) personality   (h) orbiting   (i) technique

PRESENT PARTICIPLES

- Present participles always end in 'ing'.
- Present participles often help to form a verb.

    Scientists will be **making** humans from skin cells.

- At other times present participles perform as adjectives.

    Sporting types will wear outdoor gear.

11 Write down in your books the present participles that occur in the following sentences. Next to each one say whether it is functioning as a **verb** or an **adjective.**

    (a) Parts of the oceans will be covered with floating cities in 200 years time.

    (b) They will be silent and they won't foul up the air as petrol-burning cars do.

    (c) Cars today are polluting our cities.

    (d) Scientists will be harnessing the power of the sea.

    (e) Eating habits will change too.

(f)   Work could start again in space labs orbiting the earth.

(g)   Criminals will be changing their faces to keep ahead of the police.

(h)   Life will be one long holiday with plenty of spending money.

(i)   At the moment space travel is not harming the earth.

Making present participles

The usual way of forming a present participle is just to add 'ing'. However, words ending in a single 'e' usually drop the 'e' before adding 'ing'.

live/living   provide/providing   cause/causing

Verbs which end in a single consonant preceded by a single vowel and have a stress on the final syllable, usually double the final consonant before adding 'ing'.

fit/fitting   transmit/transmitting

12 Change the words from the article into present participles:

(a)	boom	(b)	grow	(c)	permit	(d)	resist
(e)	live	(f)	supply	(g)	please	(h)	threaten
(i)	damage	(j)	travel	(k)	leave	(l)	provide
(m)	contain	(n)	improve	(o)	lead	(p)	require
(q)	cure	(r)	buy	(s)	have	(t)	dress
(u)	like	(v)	begin	(w)	ask	(x)	recreate

13 Present participles are often used as a means of **joining** sentences. Combine the following sentences by means of a present participle. Here is an example to give you the idea.

Space ships leave earth regularly. Space ships will damage the ozone layer.
Space ships leaving earth regularly will damage the ozone layer.

Decide which verb to change into a participle, and remember to leave out any words which become unnecessary. Note that the present participle of the verb 'to be' is 'being'.

(a) You take to the hairdresser a picture of a style you like. You ask him to recreate it for you.

(b) People will be able to go to their local cosmetic surgeon. They will ask him to give them a completely new face.

(c) Criminals will change their faces. They will then be able to keep ahead of the police.

(d) Crops will be grown on furrows lined with film. They will be fed by liquid manure.

(e) Cars of the future will be all electric. They will be cheaper than cars today.

(f) We have advanced storage batteries. They retain ten times as much energy as lead batteries.

(g) Scientists will also harness the power of the waves. They will extract heat from the sea.

(h) The technique is reliable. It is already used in twenty countries.

(i) Scientists will guarantee good health. They will perfect artificial organs.

(j) A depleted ozone layer would allow deadly ultra-violet rays through. Possibly the rays might cause wide-spread skin cancer.

Writers using the present participle to advantage

Often writers, wishing to make a description full of action, resort to the use of the present participle. In the scene below, a fight to the death between two dogs (White Fang and Cherokee), the writer Jack London adopts this method.

14 Read the passage through and then write down the present participles.

White Fang

White Fang was in upon him and out, ripping his trimmed remnant of an ear. With a slight display of anger, Cherokee took up the pursuit again, running on the inside of the circle White Fang was making, and striving to fasten his deadly grip on White Fang's throat. The bull-dog missed by a hair's-breadth, and cries of praise went up as White Fang doubled suddenly out of danger in the opposite direction.

The time went by. White Fang still danced on, dodging and doubling, leaping in and out, and ever inflicting damage. And still the bull-dog, with grim certitude, toiled after him. Sooner or later he would accomplish his purpose, get the grip that would win the battle.

THE PAST PARTICIPLE

The past participle usually ends in 'ed' (protected). It can also end in 'd' (heard), 'en' (fallen), or 'n' (known). Like the present participle, it can be used as part of a **verb.**

The journalist has *written* an article about the future.

Or it can be used as an **adjective.**

The hand *written* note was passed to the teacher.

A good way of working out the form of the past participle of a verb is to imagine that 'I have' comes in front of it. To work out the past participle of 'build', you think to yourself, 'I have built', and 'built' is your past participle.

15 The following sentences have been taken from the newspaper article. Write down the past participles in them.
- (a) A depleted ozone layer would allow deadly ultra-violet rays through.
- (b) Flat, windy areas will be dotted with super-efficient windmills that will store power.
- (c) They will be skilled at converting the sun's rays into electricity.
- (d) Most methods will be improved versions of techniques we use today.
- (e) Good health will be guaranteed.
- (f) Artificial organs — hearts, livers and kidneys — will be perfected.
- (g) If the Sahara were farmed like this it could feed the world.
- (h) Crops will be grown on furrows lined with film and fed by liquid manure.
- (i) But the food they eat may be made from things that we throw away today.
- (j) Parts of the oceans will be covered with floating cities.

Below is a list of verbs with their present tense, past tense, and past participle. Look closely at their past participles.

Present Tense	Past Tense	Past Participle	Present Tense	Past Tense	Past Participle
am	was	been	give	gave	given
arise	arose	arisen	go	went	gone
awake	awoke	awakened	grow	grew	grown
beat	beat	beaten	hear	heard	heard
become	became	become	hide	hid	hidden
begin	began	begun	keep	kept	kept
bend	bent	bent	kneel	knelt	knelt
bite	bit	bitten	know	knew	known
bleed	bled	bled	lay	laid	laid
blow	blew	blown	leave	left	left
break	broke	broken	lie	lay	lain
bring	brought	brought	lose	lost	lost
build	built	built	make	made	made
buy	bought	bought	meet	met	met
catch	caught	caught	pay	paid	paid
choose	chose	chosen	ride	rode	ridden
come	came	come	ring	rang	rung
do	did	done	run	ran	run
draw	drew	drawn	say	said	said
drink	drank	drunk	sell	sold	sold
drive	drove	driven	send	sent	sent
eat	ate	eaten	shake	shook	shaken
fall	fell	fallen	sing	sang	sung
feel	felt	felt	slide	slid	slid
fight	fought	fought	speak	spoke	spoken
fly	flew	flown	swim	swam	swum
forget	forgot	forgotten	tear	tore	torn
freeze	froze	frozen	write	wrote	written
get	got	got			

16 Insert the correct participle of the verb shown in brackets. Check the list on the opposite page if you are in doubt.
(a) The man has [.....] too much water. [drink]
(b) He has [.....] ten miles. [swim]
(c) The teacher has [.....] to the student. [speak]
(d) The jockey had [.....] four winners. [ride]
(e) The student had [.....] his name from the sheet. [tear]
(f) *The Silver Sword* had [.....] well [.....]. [become, know]
(g) The scientists had [.....] that the plant had [.....]. [hear, grow]
(h) The headmaster was [.....] at dawn. [awake]
(i) The [.....] child was almost [.....] by a mad dog. [lose, bite]
(j) The [.....] vase was [.....]. [break, buy]

HOMOPHONES

17 In the article there are some homophones, words that have the same sound but different spelling. Write down these sentences and put in the correct word.
(a) The sun will be a [.....] of energy. Don't put [.....] on your hot dog. [source, sauce]
(b) Of [.....] the scientists will have discovered the [.....] of cancer. [cause, course]
(c) Nightmare monsters may be [.....]. They may be able to live on [.....]. [bread, bred]
(d) The scientists will not be [.....] to pollute the earth. Don't talk [.....]. [allowed, aloud]
(e) Sporting types will [.....] sports gear. We don't know [.....] windmills will be erected. [where, wear]
(f) The scientists are quite sure [.....] methods will work and [.....] generally right. [there, their, they're]
(g) Scientists are [.....] that our living space will no longer be confined to the [.....] line. [sure, shore]
(h) Car batteries have [.....] in them. Don't be easily [.....]. [lead, led]

The Write Approach

18   Write an essay of about 25 lines on *one* of the following topics.
   (a)   It came from outer space.
   (b)   The world 200 years from now.
   (c)   My school 200 years from now.
   (d)   My home 200 years from now.
   (e)   A journey to the planets in the time machine.

Talk time

19   Do you think the mining of uranium should be allowed in Australia?

20   Do you think the motor car should be banned from cities during daylight hours?

21   How do you think people could be encouraged to use public transport?

22   Do you think we are using too many aerosol sprays? (Some scientists have suggested that excessive use of these sprays will eventually harm the ozone layer.)

23   Do you think that improvements brought about by modern technology will make us happier?

24   Discuss the statement: That the best things in life are free.

25   Do you think non-returnable containers should be banned?

26   Are you looking forward to the year 2000? Why?

One night, while he's out he could be killed.

It could happen simply because the last time you were at the Supermarket you didn't get Whiskas Litter.

It's a sad fact of life that most cats die before they're 8. Not because of natural causes. but because they're allowed out at night.

If he roams free after dark he's more susceptible to killer diseases such as feline enteritis. pneumonitis: to infectious wounds caused by dogs. other cats. even rats.

And to something a cat doesn't have a fighting chance against — fast moving traffic. It takes a deadly toll. Whiskas Litter is a safe. hygienic indoor toilet for your cat. It is now available from your local Supermarket and it will provide him with full protection from the dangers of the night. Look for it. You could be saving his life.

Whiskas Litter. Now available from your supermarket.

Check your understanding

1 What is the main argument of this advertisement?
2 What does the expression 'natural causes' mean?
3 What do you think 'unnatural causes' might be?
4 Do you think this advertisement is successful? Why?
5 Why do you think the cat in the picture was chosen?
6 If you owned a cat, what feelings would this advertisement cause you to have?
7 What do you think the words 'fighting chance' mean?
8 What feelings does the word 'rats' cause you to have?
9 Even though the advertiser realizes many of his readers will not know what 'feline enteritis' is, he still uses it. Can you explain why?
10 Write down the meaning of the following words. If you do not know their meaning or are unsure, look them up in the dictionary at the back of this book. (a) susceptible (b) infectious (c) hygienic (d) local (e) toll

HOW WELL DO YOU USE WORDS?

11 In the left-hand column are some of the words from the advertisement. Use the correct form of each word in the space in the sentence.

(a) dangers   It is dangerous for a cat to cross a street used by speeding cars.

(b) killer   The cat was almost [.....] by an approaching car.

(c) were   The cat [.....] safe inside the gate.

(d) natural   The cat was [.....] afraid of cars.

(e) protection   The workers wore [.....] clothing.

(f) provide   The owner is [.....] food for the cats.

(g) local   There are many cats in our [.....].

(h) free   Our cat has a great deal of [.....].

(i) safe   The cat ran to [.....].

(j) simply   There is a [.....] solution to the problem.

12 Find words that have been used in the advertisement by joining together their parts from the two columns below.

(a)	be	ing
(b)	dis	ly
(c)	loc	cause
(d)	simp	ease
(e)	suscept	vide
(f)	pro	ible
(g)	fight	al
(h)	avail	able

13 Fill in the following table. The last letter of the missing word has been given to help you.

	NOUN	VERB	ADJECTIVE
(a)	protection	[....t]	[....ve]
(b)	[....h]	die	[....d]
(c)	[....ty]	avail	[....e]
(d)	allowance	[....w]	[....e]
(e)	[....icity]	simplify	[....e]

THE WRITE APPROACH

14 Write a story about one of the following.
   (a) A flea's view of a cat [or any other animal you may like to use]
   (b) A day in the life of [the cat in the picture, or some other animal]
   (c) Suddenly I was transformed into [the cat in the picture]
   (d) The most [stupid, evil, intelligent, hairy, adventurous, etc.] cat on earth
   (e) The day I was taken to see the vet
   (f) How I trained my master and mistress
   (g) Why I ran away from my [kennel, hutch, stable, cage, bowl, etc.]

If you've got blackheads, oily skin or pimples, here are the only things you should squeeze.

SCRUB OUT is for blackheads and oily skin. It cleans your skin by gently scrubbing out excessive oil and skin debris, leaving your pores open and clean. Because of its formula you can actually feel SCRUB OUT working, gently cleansing your skin and helping remove blackheads wherever they appear.

FREE & CLEAR helps dry out pimples on face, chest, shoulders and back. It's a non sticky, transparent medicated gel. Guys can use it day or night. And girls can use it even under make-up.

FREE & CLEAR is greaseless and won't stain. And you only need apply FREE & CLEAR once a day. As well as being invisible on the skin it is slightly astringent and cooling. You can actually feel it starting to dry out your pimples as soon as you apply it. It tingles!

Now at leading chemists everywhere.

SCRUB OUT, for blackheads and oily skin.

FREE & CLEAR helps dry out pimples.

Check your understanding

15 This advertisement appeals to a particular need in the reader. What is this need?

16 What is the difference between the products 'Scrub Out' and 'Free & Clear'?

17 Do you think 'Scrub Out' and 'Free & Clear' are names that would help to sell the products? Why?

18 Why do you think the advertiser has repeated the word 'gently'?

19 Why does the advertiser make the point about 'Free & Clear' being invisible?

20 What arguments does the advertiser put forward for using 'Scrub Out'?

21 Will they persuade you to buy the product? Why?

22 Do you think this advertisement is a successful one? Why?

23 The language used is the language that we hear in conversation. Why has the advertiser used this kind of language?

24 How could you improve this advertisement?

25 Give the meaning of the following words. If you don't know their meaning look them up in the dictionary at the back of the book.
(a) astringent (b) debris (c) excessive (d) transparent (e) tingles

WORD FORMATIONS

26 Fill in the following table for **past** and **present** time. The first example has been done to help you. All the verbs occur in the advertisement.

	PRESENT	PAST
(a)	It dries.	It dried.
(b)	You apply.	You [.....]
(c)	It is [.....].	It was working.
(d)	It leaves.	It [.....].
(e)	They clean.	They [.....].
(f)	We are [.....].	We were helping.
(g)	They do [.....].	They appeared.
(h)	It scrubs.	It [.....].

     (i)   They lead.   They [.....].
     (j)   He needs.   He [.....].
     (k)   We [.....].   We were helping.

27 Write down the **full form** of the following words.
     (a) it's   (b) you've   (c) won't   (d) can't

28 The words in the first column have been taken from the advertisement. Each word in the other column has the **opposite** meaning to one of the words. Match up the words.

WORD	OPPOSITE
(a) day	wet
(b) free	mostly
(c) transparent	front
(d) gently	night
(e) back	captive
(f) appear	opaque
(g) invisible	roughly
(h) dry	disappear
(i) slightly	visible

29 Form the **opposites** of the following words by adding 'in', 'un', 'dis', 'im', 'il' to their beginnings or 'less' to their endings.
     (a) help   (b) grease   (c) visible   (d) common
     (e) appear   (f) legal   (g) happy   (h) patient
     (i) care   (j) even   (k) excusable

30 Change the following words from the advertisement into **nouns.**
     (a) appear   (b) apply   (c) clean   (d) remove
     (e) clear   (f) invisible   (g) open   (h) sticky

31 Change the following words from the advertisement into **adjectives.**
     (a) face   (b) day   (c) actually   (d) pimple   (e) gently

32 Verbs, nouns and adjectives from the advertisement have been mixed up. Sort them into three columns under the headings, **nouns, verbs, adjectives.**

cleans	debris	formula	remove
sticky	girls	day	astringent
pimples	oily	chemists	excessive
face	invisible	chest	got
things	are	transparent	should

THE WRITE APPROACH

33 Imagine that you have just invented one of the following products. Now write a radio or newspaper advertisement to sell your product.
(a) a cure for baldness   (b) a new breakfast food
(c) a new lipstick   (d) a new pet food
(e) a cure for headaches and colds   (f) a new ice cream flavour
(g) a product of your own choice

34 Write a TV commercial that can be acted out in front of the class. You may like to copy an existing commercial.

35 Select three advertisements that have appeared on TV, radio or in a newspaper. Briefly outline each advertisement and then explain what approach the advertiser is using to try and sell the product.

36 Select something that you really like and write an advertisement to try and sell it. (Your favourite tennis racquet, your Dolly magazines, your favourite icecream, your favourite clothes, your favourite food, etc.)

TALK TIME

37 Why do you think the 'Scrub Out' and 'Free & Clear' advertisement would appeal to young people? What do you like about the advertisement?

38 What do you dislike about the advertisement?

39 What do you think about television advertising?

40 What is your favourite television advertisement? Explain to the class why you like it.

41 Which influences you most: your family, your school, television, radio, the newspaper, the church, or advertising? Why?

42 Should advertising be reduced, abolished, or reformed?

43 Comment on an advertisement that has annoyed you.

44 Comment on an advertisement that you feel has misled or deceived you.

45 Examine the old advertisement for the Magic Washer. Find a modern advertisement to compare with it.

Unit Nine: Cure

The germ killer

Even though he was getting old (he was now sixty), he did not stop working. He couldn't; for Louis, his work had always been his life. He slowed down a little, but only a little. Now he turned his attention to a new disease, a strange disease called rabies. It affects dogs and, through them, human beings. When a dog has rabies he is called 'rabid,' or mad. In this condition he foams at the mouth and often bites people. When a person is bitten by a mad dog, he may get rabies himself, but not until four weeks later. It is a long, painful disease. Before Pasteur's work on it, the person who was bitten by one of these 'mad dogs' usually died.

No one knew the cause of rabies or its cure. Pasteur decided that he would find out. Very shortly he discovered that he had taken on the hardest job of his life.

To begin with, Pasteur could not find the microbe that was responsible. 'It must be there,' Pasteur muttered, bending down and peering into his microscope. 'If only I can find it.' Finally he decided that the germ was too small to see even with a microscope.

One day as Pasteur sat in his laboratory looking at the rabid dogs in their cages around him, he thought, 'There is one thing about rabies that is very strange. It takes so long to get it after a person is bitten — almost a month. If only there were some way to prevent the disease from growing immediately after the person is bitten, then we would have a real cure.'

Suddenly, the howling of one of the mad dogs interrupted his thoughts. He watched as the dog jumped at him, stopped only by the bars of its cage. This was dangerous work that Pasteur was doing. The mad dogs themselves were highly dangerous; even their spit was threatening, since it carried the invisible rabies germs. Louis and his assistants had to be very careful.

As time passed, Pasteur found a way to weaken rabies germs. When he injected these germs into healthy dogs they did not get sick. Finally he put the inoculated dogs into cages with the rabid animals. The healthy dogs were bitten savagely. But, as time passed, Pasteur kept on with his treatment of the normal animals. They did not get sick.

It seemed that Pasteur had found a way to prevent rabies in dogs by giving them repeated doses of the weak germs. Perhaps he had beaten rabies as well as anthrax!

Then one day a little boy was brought into Pasteur's laboratory by his mother.

'How do you do?' Pasteur rose from his laboratory stool. 'What can I do for you?'

'We have come to you for help,' said the woman desperately. 'My little boy, Joseph, has been badly bitten by a mad dog. Our doctor thought that you could help us. He says that there is nothing he can do.'

Pasteur looked at the little boy; the child was in pain and could hardly walk. But Pasteur had never tried his treatment on human beings. He had no idea if it would work. It might hurt the boy instead of saving him. If the boy died, people would call Pasteur a criminal. What should he do? It was the most difficult decision of his life.

Pasteur said, 'Come back this afternoon. I must think about it.'

Pasteur then went out to talk to some doctors about the child. They all told him, 'Go ahead. The case is so serious that there is nothing to lose.'

Later in the afternoon, when Joseph and his mother returned,

Pasteur began the treatment. Before Pasteur gave Joseph the weakened germs, Joseph had been sobbing uncontrollably. Afterward he grew calm. His mother put him to bed and he slept easily. But Pasteur got very little rest. Anxiously, he waited for morning. When he saw that Joseph was still all right, he regained a little of his confidence.

The treatments continued for the next ten days. They were, for Pasteur, the longest ten days of his life. In the middle of the night, he would awake with a start, expecting the worst news of all — that the child had died. When he did sleep, he had dreams of Joseph's getting sick. His fears were groundless. Each morning Joseph seemed to be getting better.

At the end of the ten days there was nothing further that Pasteur could do. Louis was exhausted, physically and mentally. Still unsure of his success, he went to the country to rest. He still dreaded a telegram telling him that something had gone wrong.

The telegram never came. A month went by. The boy had recovered. Pasteur had indeed found a cure for rabies!

JOHN MANN, *The Germ Killer*

Check your understanding

1 How does a dog behave when he has rabies?
2 What is one of the unusual features of rabies for a human, when bitten?
3 What was the first difficulty Pasteur experienced with the rabies microbe?
4 How did Pasteur believe he might eventually defeat rabies?
5 Why was the spit of the mad dogs very dangerous?
6 How did Pasteur test that his rabies treatment for dogs was successful?
7 Why was Pasteur worried about trying his new treatment on Joseph?
8 Why did Pasteur finally decide to try his treatment on Joseph?
9 How do you know that Pasteur was worried while Joseph was being treated?

10 Write down the meaning of the following words. If you don't know their meaning or are unsure, look them up in the dictionary at the back of your book.

(a) peering   (b) inoculated   (c) exhausted   (d) confidence

ADVERBS USED WITH VERBS

Just as adjectives tell us more about nouns, so one of the important jobs of adverbs is to add to the meaning of verbs. These kinds of adverbs often, but not always, end in 'ly'. Adverbs used with verbs generally occur under the three headings below.

● **Manner** (How)
Adverbs used with verbs may tell **how** an action is done.

He walked *slowly* into school

'Slowly' tells how he walked into school.

quickly	happily	easily	carefully
bravely	loudly	slowly	noiselessly
violently	anxiously	savagely	fast

● **Time** (When)
Adverbs used with verbs may tell **when** an action is done.

He comes home *early* from school.

'Early' tells when he comes home from school.

now	early	later	then
again	often	previously	today
yesterday	seldom	sometimes	already

● **Place** (Where)
Adverbs used with verbs may tell **where** an action is done.

He has looked *there*.

'There' tells where he has looked.

here	there	everywhere	anywhere
somewhere	forward	backward	far
near	down	up	nowhere

Find the adverbs

11 Find the adverbs in the sentences below, which have been taken from the story. Write them down with their verbs. Draw up two columns with the headings 'adverbs,' 'verbs'.

    (a) In this condition he foams at the mouth and often bites people.

    (b) The healthy dogs were bitten savagely.

    (c) For Louis, his work had always been his life.

    (d) Very shortly he discovered that he had taken on the hardest job of his life.

    (e) Suddenly, the howling of one of the mad dogs interrupted his thoughts.

    (f) Finally he decided that the germ was too small to see even with a microscope.

    (g) 'We have come to you for help,' said the woman desperately.

    (h) 'My little boy, Joseph, has been badly bitten by a mad dog.'

    (i) The child was in pain and could hardly walk.

    (j) Later in the afternoon, when Joseph and his mother returned, Pasteur began the treatment.

12 Writers sometimes begin sentences with adverbs to give their writing variation and make their sentences more interesting or to draw attention to a particular adverb. Find at least four sentences in the story that begin with adverbs and write them into your books.

13 The following sentences from the story have been rearranged so that they now begin with adverbs. Write their new beginnings down and complete their endings.

    (a) Louis was exhausted, physically and mentally. Physically and mentally . . .

    (b) His mother put him to bed and he slept easily. Easily he slept after . . .

(c) For Louis his work had always been his life. Always Louis's work . . .

(d) Write three sentences of your own starting with adverbs.

14 Below are some of the adverbs from the story. See whether you can find the six that have their letters scrambled up.

often   immediately   suddenly   desperately
uncontrollably   anxiously   mentally   physically
savagely   finally   usually   easily

(a) u u l y s a l
(b) e p s e d a r l y e t
(c) s i e l a y
(d) s i a l y n o x u
(e) l y s d e d n u
(f) t i e m d i m a e l y

15 Fill in the missing letters and write the adverbs into your books.
(a) p..s.c..ly
(b) .f..n
(c) ..s.ly
(d) ..v.g.ly
(e) .s..ll.
(f) ..s..r.t.ly

16 Here is a list of adjectives from the story. Change them into adverbs. They all will end in 'ly', but sometimes you will have to add other letters or drop a letter.
(a) dangerous
(b) repeated
(c) human
(d) painful
(e) responsible
(f) final
(g) personal
(h) threatening
(i) invisible
(j) normal
(k) sick
(l) serious
(m) successful

Blankety adverbs

17 The following passage from *Coral Island* has a number of blank spaces. Write out the passage, and from the box beneath select adverbs to fit the blanks. Some adverbs will fit in more than one

space, but you can only use each word in the box *once*. The passage will only read well if you have the right adverb in the right space. Sometimes the first letter of the missing word has been given to help you.

> immediately   over   now   strongly   afterwards
> then   here   close   away   suddenly
> distinctly   before   doubtlessly

Coral Island

We [n.....] saw the shark quite [d.....] swimming round and round us, its sharp fin every now and [.....] thrusting itself above the water. From its active and unsteady movements, Jack knew that it was making up its mind to attack us, so he urged us [.....] to paddle for our lives, while he himself set the example. [S.....] he shouted, 'Look out! [.....] he comes!', and in a second we saw the monstrous fish dive [c.....] under us, and turn half [.....] on his side. But we all made a great commotion with our paddles, which [.....] frightened it [.....] for that time, as we saw it [i.....] circling round us as [.....].

Select the correct word

18 Insert the correct word from the two words in the brackets.

(a) A person with rabies [.....] endures it for a month. [painful, painfully]

(b) Pasteur worked [.....] to find a cure for rabies. [good, well]

(c) The disease grew [.....] after a person was bitten. [slowly, slow]

(d) Joseph's mother was [.....]. [desperately, desperate]

(e) Louis and his assistant [.....] kept their bodies away from the bars of the cage. [carefully, careful]

(f) Pasteur was [.....] about the boy's health. [anxious, anxiously]

(g) Pasteur's sleep was not [.....]. [peacefully, peaceful]

(h) Pasteur had indeed [.....] cured rabies. [successfully, successful]

ALPHABETICAL ADVERBS

19   This game can be played around the class. Each person must think of an adverb which describes how the chicken crossed the road. However, the first person's adverb must begin with the letter 'a', the next with 'b', and so on right through the alphabet. (Don't worry about the letter 'x' — go straight on to 'y'.)
The chicken crossed the road **a**ngrily

badly

cautiously

dangerously

endlessly

THE WRITE APPROACH

20   Write an essay with the title, 'Why modern inventions are important in my life'.

21   Select an object or something that you use, and explain how it works to someone who wants to use it.
(a) the safety pin, (b) a washing machine, (c) a lawn mower, (d) hair dryer, (e) a sewing machine, (f) a calculator, (g) a dictionary, (h) a telephone, (i) a record player, (j) a bicycle, (k) a motorbike, (l) an alarm clock, (m) a typewriter.

22   Describe your hobby or the sport you like best to someone who is interested in getting involved.

TALK TIME

23   Which do you think is the greatest invention of the following?
(a) the motor car, (b) the telephone, (c) television, (d) the aeroplane, (e) the electric light.

24   Which do you think is the most useful invention of the following?
(a) false teeth, (b) glasses, (c) scissors, (d) the watch , (e) the razor blade.

Unit Ten: Elephant

Elephants of the Congo

It happened when I was driving across the Rwindi plain, on the lookout for suitable animals for the camera team to film later in the day. About a kilometre from the road, across some extremely rough country, I saw a very big elephant. He was a fine old tusker and he was alone.

Now, it is not a bad rule, if you wish to observe large game animals and stay alive, to avoid the old isolated one and stick to the herd. This is especially the case with elephants. In old age the head of the herd becomes driven out by his successor; he is often the one who gets a bad name as a rogue elephant and he is usually more aggressive and difficult to deal with than the rest of the herd.

Of course, I heard all this several times, but the sight of this great elephant, so close and apparently so peaceful, was too much to resist. I had a loaded portable 35 mm camera with me, so I stopped the car and cheerfully set out after the elephant on foot. Downwind of him ran a fairly substantial range of bushes. I judged that if I could once get behind them and then work towards him, I would be able to get some really exciting close-ups of the old monster.

All this seemed to work very well. I got behind one end of the bushes without being spotted and worked forward. But by the time I had got to the front of the clump and parted the branches, I saw that the elephant had come closer as well, and was now less than twenty metres away. This was better than I could ever have expected, except for one thing. From where I was sitting, there was yet another small bush directly in my line of vision that kept getting into the picture, no matter how I moved.

Finally, I decided to risk it. The elephant seemed more concerned with the foliage he was eating than with me, so I stepped out into the open, sighted my camera, and prepared to take some of the best pictures of my life of a big tusker at close quarters.

It was the clicking of my camera that did it. As soon as he heard the noise, out went his ears, up went his trunk, and I could see him feeling the air, listening for the next sound.

Curiously, the fact that I was so patently visible did not matter.

To any other animal, I would have been as large as a house, but elephants have poor eyesight and at that age rarely notice things that stand still. At least, I had the sense not to move.

But trouble began the instant I stopped the camera. It was the change of sound that presumably irritated him and told him where I was. Determinedly he started moving towards me. I moved away. He accelerated and then at last I realized that I was actually in danger. This was the beginning of a charge.

It was then that I started to run in earnest, but to my horror I found that I could hardly move, because the ground was so rough, whereas this scarcely bothered him at all. He came lumbering on, unerringly on my track by now, and there was nothing I could do except blunder hopelessly forward clutching my camera.

Then, incredibly, he stopped and I looked back. He was standing on the exact spot where I had been when I filmed him. Obviously he had got my scent so strong that he thought I was still there. He was going exclusively by scent and hearing, not by sight, and soon started pounding the ground there with his great feet and charging with his tusks. It was then I noticed what I should have seen earlier on: his far tusk was broken half-way off. This is a bad sign with an elephant. He may have broken it off in a fight or by hitting a tree; if the nerve was exposed, he may have suffered a painful abscess. It is always best to give a wide berth to an elephant with a broken tusk, as his behaviour is likely to be abnormal and unpredictable.

The one thing that probably saved my life was his weak eyesight. I managed to cover a good fifty metres before it struck him that it was only earth he was pounding, not me. Twice more this happened on the way back to the car. Twice more he got my scent and started to pound the ground. Thanks to this, I made it, but only just. When I reached the car the old elephant was not far behind me, and it was lucky the car started first time, for the car was something that even he could see. Once I had got going I kept at top speed for the next 15 kilometres.

ARMAND DENIS, *On Safari*

Check your understanding

1 What rule did Denis fail to observe when he decided to film the elephant?

2 Why was Denis particularly tempted to film the elephant?

3 Why did Denis wish to be downwind of the elephant?

4 Why did Denis decide that he could risk making himself visible to the elephant?

5 What made the elephant aware of Denis's presence?

6 What difficulty did Denis experience in trying to move away from the elephant?

7 Why did the elephant stop?

8 Why is it best to avoid an elephant with a broken tusk?

9 What evidence can you find to support Denis's statement that 'the one thing that probably saved my life was his (the elephant's) weak eyesight'?

10 What did you learn about Denis's character from this story?

11 What is the meaning of the following words? You may need to use the dictionary at the back of the book.
(a) accelerated   (b) blunder   (c) clump   (d) incredibly

WORD MEANINGS

12 Write down the words in the left-hand column. Then write down their meanings after you have found them in the right-hand column.

WORD	MEANING
(a) isolated	leaves
(b) aggressive	convenient for carrying
(c) rogue	a considerable number
(d) pounding	attacking
(e) portable	alone
(f) substantial	evil tempered
(g) foliage	moving clumsily
(h) patently	straight
(i) unerringly	thumping
(j) lumbering	clearly

ADVERBS OF DEGREE

You have seen some examples of how adverbs extend the meaning of verbs. However, adverbs have another job. They may also add to the meaning of adjectives and other adverbs. Most of these adverbs fall under the heading of adverbs of **degree**.

The student was **very** quiet in class.

The adverb 'very' adds to the meaning of the adjective 'quiet'.

The student was speaking **rather** quietly.

The adverb 'rather' adds to the meaning of the adverb 'quietly'.

Now look at the box of some of the typical adverbs of **degree**.

very	almost	more	most	rather	only	quite
exceedingly	so	sufficiently	too	fairly	really	

13 Find the adverbs of degree in the following sentences. Next to them write down the adjectives or adverbs they add meaning to.

(a) Downwind of him ran a fairly substantial range of bushes.

(b) All this seemed to work very well.

(c) I would be able to get some really exciting close-ups of the old monster.

(d) The elephant seemed more concerned with the foliage he was eating than with me.

(e) Across some extremely rough country, I saw a very big elephant.

14 The jumbled letters can be sorted into adverbs from the degree box. Write down the sentences.

(a) The writer, Armand Denis was [nixdeeceylg] anxious when he tried to start his car.

(b) The elephant had [yerv] poor eyesight.

(c) A rogue elephant is usually [reom] aggressive and difficult to deal with than the rest of the herd.

(d) The elephant was [oto] concerned with the foliage he was eating to notice the photographer twenty metres away.

(e) An elephant with a broken tusk is [aleyrl] dangerous.

15 Find the adverbs in the story that have a **similar** meaning to the words in the left-hand column. The first letter of the word has been given to help you.

    (a) with skill   s.....

    (b) with curiosity   c.....

    (c) at the end   f.....

    (d) generally   u.....

    (e) happily   c.....

    (f) with determination d.....

    (g) really   a.....

    (h) barely   s.....

    (i) without hope   h.....

    (j) unbelievingly   i.....

    (k) clearly   o.....

16 Write down the following sentences and in the spaces insert the most suitable adverb from those in the brackets.

    (a) The cameraman ..... set out after the elephant on foot. [worriedly, hastily, cheerfully]

    (b) The elephant ..... chased after Denis. [silently, determinedly, sadly]

    (c) A rogue elephant tends to act ...... [happily, lovingly, aggressively]

    (d) Denis had acted ..... in trying to film the rogue elephant. [rashly, thoughtfully, clumsily]

    (e) When Denis started his car, he drove ..... for fifteen kilometres. [carefully, speedily, bravely]

Put the adverbs back together

17 In the tables below are adverbs from the story, but their parts are mixed up. Take a part from column 1, a part from column 2, and a part from column 3 to find your adverb.

	COLUMN 1	COLUMN 2	COLUMN 3
(a)	pro	clusive	ly
(b)	ob	cred	ly

COLUMN 1	COLUMN 2	COLUMN 3
(c) pre	ect	ly
(d) hope	sum	ably
(e) in	less	ially
(f) dir	spec	ly
(g) e	treme	ly
(h) ex	vious	ibly
(i) ex	bab	ly

18 Take a part from column 1 and a part from column 2 to find your adverb.

COLUMN 1	COLUMN 2
(a) for	ier
(b) fin	ly
(c) of	ly
(d) fair	ually
(e) us	ten
(f) hard	ward
(g) earl	ly
(h) like	ally

Put the adverbs in the correct spaces

19 Rider Haggard in his book *King Solomon's Mines* also describes an encounter with an elephant. Like Armand Denis, he makes use of adverbs to make his story realistic. In the passage below the adverbs have been taken out and placed in the box above the passage. Write out the passage and insert the adverbs in their correct positions. Sometimes the first letter of the missing adverb has been given to you.

Loose adverbs

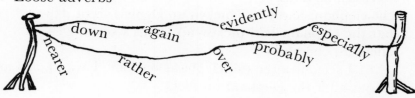

King Solomon's Mines

The solitary bull stood fifty metres or so this side of the herd, over which he was [e.....] keeping sentry, and about sixty metres from us. Thinking that he would see or wind us, and that it would [.....] start them all [o.....] [.....] if we tried to get [.....], [e.....] as the ground was [r.....] open, we all aimed at this bull, and at my whispered word fired. All three shots took effect, and [.....] he went, dead.

Telling the difference between adjectives and adverbs

20   An adjective adds meaning to a noun. An adverb adds meaning to a verb, adjective or another adverb. Keeping these facts in mind, write down the sentences below and put in the correct word.

(a)   [unpredictable, unpredictably]
       The elephant behaved [.....]. The elephant's behaviour was unpredictable.

(b)   [determined, determinedly]
       He was [.....] as he moved towards me. He [.....] moved towards me.

(c)   [extreme, extremely]
       The elephant's abscess was [.....] painful. The pain of the elephant's abscess was [.....].

(d)   [probable, probably]
       It seemed [.....] that the elephant's weak eyesight saved Denis's life. The elephant's weak eyesight [.....] saved Denis's life.

(e)   [aggressive, aggressively]
       The elephant moved [.....] towards Denis. The elephant's movement was [.....].

(f)   [obvious, obviously]
       The elephant had [.....] picked up Denis's scent. It was [.....] that the elephant had picked up Denis's scent.

(g)   [cheerful, cheerfully]
       I [.....] set out after the elephant on foot. I was [.....] as I set out after the elephant on foot.

(h) [incredible, incredibly]
His stopping seemed [.....]. [.....] he stopped.

(i) [lucky, luckily]
[.....] the car started first time. It was [.....] the car started first time.

(j) [direct, directly]
A small bush was in the cameraman's [.....] line of vision. There was a small bush [.....] in the cameraman's line of vision.

Write down the opposites of the adverbs

21 The words in the left-hand column are adverbs that have been taken from the story. Write them down in your books. Then next to them, write down words that are opposite in meaning. The first letter(s) has been given to help you.

(a) forward   b.....
(b) towards   aw.....
(c) here   t.....
(d) rarely   al.....
(e) hopelessly   hopef.....
(f) strongly   w.....
(g) earlier   l.....
(h) often   n.....
(i) more   l.....
(j) cheerfully   s.....

THE WRITE APPROACH

22 Choose one of the following topics and write about twenty-five lines on it.

(a) A lion at school!
(b) Animals that I like.
(c) Animals that I am afraid of.
(d) The ideal zoo.
(e) A day in the life of..... (Select an animal.)

23 Describe your feelings and attitudes to the lionesses in the photograph.

TALK TIME

24 Many creatures such as the wedgetailed eagle and certain kinds of whales are in danger of becoming extinct. Do you think they should be saved? How can they be saved?

25 Strange as it may seem, even the crocodile in certain countries is in danger of becoming extinct. Keeping in mind that the crocodile kills man, do you think it should be a protected species? Why?

26 Should creatures like lions, panthers and elephants be kept in zoos?

Unit Eleven: Survival

Girl against the jungle

On Christmas Eve 1971 an aircraft carrying 92 people vanished without trace over the wild forestland of Peru. After breaking up in mid-air, it had crashed, scattering victims and wreckage over a large area. It was a foregone conclusion that nobody could have survived. Yet after ten days, a seventeen-year-old girl emerged from the jungle, the sole survivor. Only by sheer guts did she come through her ordeal, and her story is all the more remarkable for the calm way in which it is told.

I've always liked flying, and never been afraid in the air. So I felt very carefree as I boarded the plane with my mother at Lima. It was Christmas Eve. We were going to Pucallpa, up in the jungle, to join my father, and we knew he had prepared a Christmas tree to welcome us.

I was still not worried when the plane — a Lockheed Electra — did not take off until 11.15 a.m. It had been due to start at seven, but in Peru planes are rarely on time, so you become used to it. There were more than 80 passengers, but I managed to get a window seat, in row 19 on the right. Everything was normal: taking-off, curving over the Pacific, gaining height, crossing the Andes, a meal, the smiles of the stewardesses. We saw the snow-covered peaks of the Andes and then the jungle that stretched right up to the horizon in the east. Some of the passengers were asleep as the stewardesses collected the breakfast trays, still smiling.

Then rain began pattering against the window panes, and the aircraft was thrown about vertically. There were the first screams from the passengers.

I looked out into the clouds and saw lightning; it was dangerously near. We should have reached Pucallpa long ago. Again the aircraft was rocking violently, there were more screams, and some hand luggage fell off the racks.

'This is the end,' said my mother. She had been afraid of flying ever since she had experienced a bad storm on a flight somewhere over the United States. But this time her fear was not caused by the shaking of the plane — it was also on fire.

I saw the flames. Bright yellow, they shot out of the right wing. I looked over to my mother, but at the same moment there was a tremendous jolt that passed right through the aircraft. The next thing I realized was that I was no longer inside the plane. I was outside. I was sitting in the open air on my seat. I was flying through the air.

I remember that I could hardly breathe because the seat-belt was pressing on my stomach. I also remember that I was turning round and round in the air. And I remember finally that the trees of the jungle underneath looked like cauliflower, lots and lots of cauliflower. Then I lost consciousness.

I was woken up by the rain. It was pouring down as hard as it can only pour during the rainy season in this part of the world. There was thunder, and it was still daylight.

I was lying under my seat, but the seat next to mine was empty. there was no trace of my mother, and no trace of a man who had sat on my mother's left and had still been fast asleep when the plane had made that tremendous jolt. I couldn't see any trace of the plane — I was all alone, with only the croaking of frogs and the chirping of insects. Looking around, I saw I was lying in a forest, that grew on slightly sloping ground.

Strange as it may sound, the truth is that I did not feel very much. I simply registered that my seat-belt had gone, that I had lost a shoe, a ring that had been a present from my mother, and my glasses. My 'hippie' mini-dress did not seem to be torn and I felt very astonished about it. A bone was sticking out oddly from underneath my neck, and I wondered if it was my collar bone. One of my eyes was swollen, I had a bump on my head and a small wound on my foot. I was not in pain, but I did not have the strength to get up and look around. So I remained lying under the seat all night, half asleep and dazed.

Dazed, and with only a few sweets to keep her from starving, she begins walking away from the crash.

On the second day my injuries still did not hurt me, nor on the third. Instead my back began to hurt — it had grown badly sun-burnt. The fastening at the back of my dress was broken and through the trees the sun had caught me. In the Peruvian jungle the sun is as brutal as the rain — people from temperate climates of Europe are not equal to either of them.

But in spite of the pain on my back I covered much more ground on the third day, after a good night's rest. I had the feeling that I had got stronger, though I lived on nothing but a few sweets and water. Of course, I was constantly bitten by mosquitoes and horse flies that were impossible to get rid of, but I did not care about that. I did not realize that with every sting the flies deposited underneath my skin their eggs, from which the larvae would creep out later on.

Her one plan is to follow jungle streams down to a big river where there might be someone living. However, soon the insects begin to take their dreadful toll.

The mosquitoes and flies never left me — always the mosquitoes and flies. The wound on my foot had grown worse because of the insects. I should have removed the flies' eggs from under my skin, but I had no tweezers, nothing with which to get them out. So I had to let those horrible larvae grow until they pushed their wobbly heads through the skin.

The hope I had put on the bigger river was soon dashed. I realized that I was far from any human habitation because of the way the animals I encountered behaved — they were not afraid of me. The moment that dawned on me I was really frightened for the first time, because the flies had stung me so badly that my arms, with the larvae growing out of them, looked dreadful.

'My God,' I thought, 'they will have to amputate one of my arms — if I survive at all.'

Next, my arm began to swell, and for the first time I began to feel pain. Really terrible pain.

I couldn't really feel very much from my collar bone, which I knew now was broken, or the fairly large wound on my foot. Even my swollen eyes, and the bumps on my head caused by the crash, did not bother me too badly. I just had to grit my teeth for the pain in my arm.

It was covered with fly bites, from which maggots were now appearing like asparagus tips from a jar. I had to do something. I must try to operate on myself.

In the crash I had lost the ring my mother had given me, but I was still wearing another ring — a spiral one — which I could snap into sharp pieces. I shaped it as a knife and used it to scratch out the dozens of maggots from my arms and legs. Every maggot was at least a centimetre long and two millimetres thick; and they were eating me alive.

At last she reaches a big river and recalls the words of her father.

The river which I had eventually found after so much agony was quite wide and had such a strong current that it often swept me off my feet. It just carried me along, and I knew how to swim. I had learnt well before 1967, when I went with my parents to live in the jungle.

'You never know,' my father said at the time, 'you never know if some day you might have to swim for your life in a river in the jungle.'

And, finally, she is rescued on the river bank.

My right arm was getting worse and again I began to worry that it would have to be amputated if I did not get help soon.

And then I heard voices from the forest. And I saw them coming. Three men, in shorts and barefooted. They spoke Spanish with a strange accent. Then they saw me. Ten and a half days after the crash that started it all, a human being talked to me again for the first time. 'Hey there,' he said. 'Who's sitting there?'

JULIANE KOEPCKE, *Girl Against the Jungle*

Check your understanding

1 Copy this report into your workbook and fill in the details from the passage.

Date of crash:
Type of aircraft:
Number of passengers:
Aircraft vanished over:
Where flight began:
Time the flight actually began:
Survivor's name:
Age:
Reason for survival:

---

2   Here is a sketch of the plane's flight seen from side on, or in cross-section. Draw this sketch in your workbook.

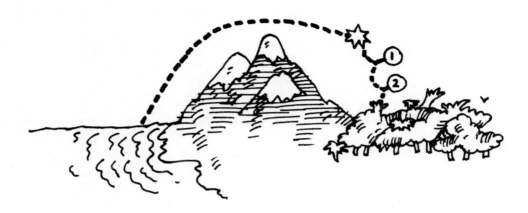

Now put down the answers to the following questions in the places where they fit best on the sketch.

(a)   Name the sea.

(b)   Name the mountain range.

(c)   At the point marked * on the sketch, complete this description: 'Bright yellow ..... aircraft.'

(d)   In your own words, what happens at point (1) and point (2) on your sketch?

(e)   When seen from above, what is the jungle like? (Write it above the trees.)

3   Answer these questions in your workbook.

(a)   What was she woken by?

(b)   Where was she when she woke?

(c)   Where was her mother? The other passengers? The plane?

(d)   She was all alone except for what?

(e)   She takes stock of herself. List what she has lost. List her injuries.

(f)   However, there's at least one thing she can be thankful for. What is it?

4 Sketch a river like the one below in your workbook. Read the questions, and **answer them on your sketch** in the places you provide.

(a) *The second day:* Her injuries are not troubling her as much as her back. Why is her back troubling her?

(b) *By the third day:* A terrible danger is creeping up on her, though she does not realize it. What is the danger?

(c) *In the days that followed:* 'The mosquitoes and flies never left me.....' What horrible things happen to her as a result? (Describe what happens in your own words.)
What does she do to rid herself of them?

(d) *As she tries to cope with the river:* What words spoken by her father seem to come true for her? (Write down the exact words.)

(e) *At last, on the river bank:* Juliane Koepcke is finally rescued by [.....].
How many days after the crash?
What are the first words she hears?

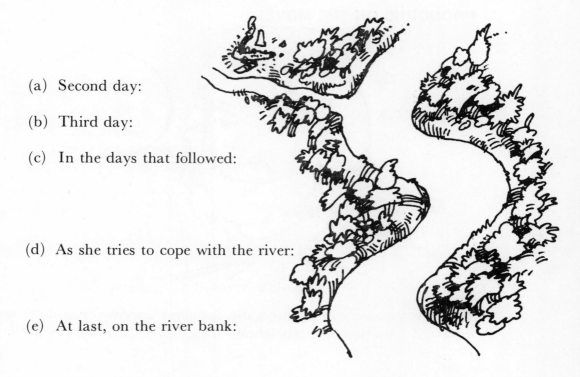

(a) Second day:

(b) Third day:

(c) In the days that followed:

(d) As she tries to cope with the river:

(e) At last, on the river bank:

SPELLING SPOT

5 Write down the following list of words from the passage, filling in the dots as you go.

(a) w.e.kage   (b) s.rv.v.r
(c) pa..en.e.s   (d) ho.iz.n
(e) v..l.nt.y   (f) m.squ.t..s
(g) con..io.sn.ss   (h) h.b.t.tion
(i) op.r.te   (j) ac.e.t

6 Write down the **plural** form of the following words.
Note: Check back in the passage to find the difficult ones!

(a) stewardess   (b) mosquito
(c) fly   (d) larva
(e) tooth   (f) crash
(g) dress   (h) tweezers
(i) knife   (j) flame

PRONOUNS ON THE MOVE!

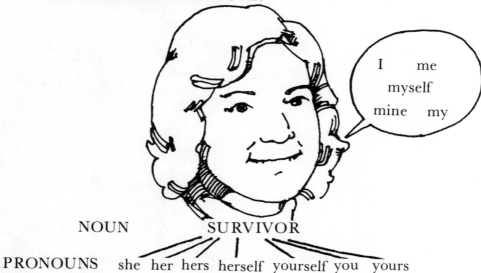

I   me
myself
mine   my

NOUN   SURVIVOR

PRONOUNS   she her hers herself yourself you   yours

These are just some of the pronouns the noun 'survivor' might rely on to save it from dreaded **overwork**!

Look at *this* hopeless situation:

> The *survivor* of the air crash had the choice of staying where the *survivor* was or of moving the *survivor* away from the area. The choice was the *survivor's* and the *survivor's* alone. The *survivor* stumbled away with the *survivor's* terrible ordeal in front of the *survivor*.

Notice how boring the word 'survivor' becomes after a few repeats! It's a fearful victim of overwork. Now compare it with this:

> The survivor of the air crash had the choice of staying where *she* was or of moving *herself* away from the area. The choice was *hers* and *hers* alone. She stumbled away with *her* terrible ordeal in front of *her*.

Here we do have some variety! Only the first 'survivor' is necessary. All the rest can be handled by pronouns.

The first 'survivor' is necessary because we need to be sure that all the pronouns really do stand in for some noun or nouns — in this case the noun 'survivor'. This is what it would be like if the pronouns lost their noun:

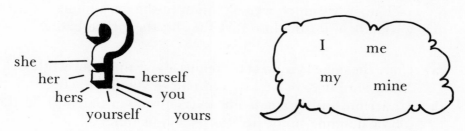

Just remember that the word **proNOUN** itself includes **NOUN** in its package deal.

7 Put the pronouns back properly into this passage:

> her   she   it   she

> 'This is the end,' said my mother. [.....] had been afraid of flying ever since [.....] had experienced a bad storm on a flight somewhere over the United States. But this time [.....] fear was not caused by the shaking of the plane — [.....] was also on fire.

8 Write down the nouns that are being stood in for. Beside each noun, write down the stand-in pronoun or pronouns.

JOBS FOR PRONOUNS

he	us	his	ours	we	it	theirs	mine
hers	she	me	yourselves		yourself	they	I
itself	himself	myself	her		themselves	you
its	yours	ourselves	them		him	herself	you
yours

Different pronouns do different jobs. Let's take a closer look at some of these different jobs.

First job

● Some pronouns stand in for *one* person or thing. They are **singular.**
   'But now I had run out of sweets.'
   'I' stands in for Juliane Koepcke, the girl against the jungle.
● Other pronouns stand in for *more than one* person or thing. They are **plural**.
   'They were much worse than even the mosquitoes.'
   'They' stands in for the blowflies that bit the girl so badly.

9 (a) Copy the mixed group of pronouns above into your workbook. Make sure they're well spaced out — you'll see why!
   (b) Underline with a single line every pronoun that will do the job of standing in for just *one* person or thing.
   (c) Underline with a double line all the pronouns that will stand for *more than one* person or thing. (Note: watch out for the **you/ yours** trap. You/yours can stand in for either one person being spoken to or a number of people being spoken to such as a class or a crowd, or even just two people being spoken to.)

Second job

● Some pronouns stand in for female nouns. Look back at the picture of the survivor. Note the specially female pronouns (e.g. 'her').
● On the other hand, some stand in for male nouns (e.g. 'he').

- Some pronouns will stand in for either female or male (e.g. 'mine').
- And, there are a couple of pronouns that stand in for things rather than people (e.g. 'it').

10 Return to the mixed group of pronouns you have put down and underlined in your workbook. Decide whether each pronoun is
   - female (F)
   - male (M)
   - either male or female (M/F)
   - a thing rather than a person (T).

After each pronoun write (F), (M), (M/F) or (T).

Third job

So far we've seen pronouns standing in for a single person, or people; or a thing or things. We've also seen them standing in for females and/ or males. The *same* pronouns can also do the job of standing in for:

- The person or people speaking (e.g. 'I', 'we'). This is called the **first person.**
- The person or people being spoken to (e.g. 'you'). This is called the **second person.**
- The person or thing, or the people or things being spoken about (e.g. 'she', 'it'). This is called the **third person.**

You are the person being spoken to (2nd person)

I am the person speaking (1st person)

She is the person being spoken about (3rd person)

Here's a table that sorts pronouns according to whether they stand in for **speaking, spoken to,** or **spoken about** nouns.

PRONOUNS		
SPEAKING (1st person)	SPOKEN TO (2nd person)	SPOKEN ABOUT (3rd person)
A	**B**	**C**
me	you	it
I	you	it
me	you	he
I		us
I		it
I		them
me		they
me		he
I		they
I		it
we		
I		
I		
I		
we		

All the pronouns in this table will fit into blanks somewhere in the passages below. Notice the bold black letters beside the blanks. Use these letters to direct you to column **A**, column **B** or column **C** in the table. Then, search the column for the pronoun that *fits* — the one that makes most sense! Here's how it works:

> But those rough bandages did not help very much to stop the bites getting infected and spreading. And [.....**C**] did not help at all to keep the insects off [.....**A**] — [.....**A**] was covered by [.....**C**].

In the first blank we obviously need a stand in for 'bandages'. **C** directs us to column **C** as the 'bandages' are being **spoken about**. The pronoun 'they' makes most sense. And, we go on to deal with 'me' **speaking**, 'I' **speaking** and 'them' **spoken about** in columns **A, A** and **C**. Got the idea? Then here are your passages. Write them in your work book, putting in the pronouns as you go.

11   [.....**A**] 've always liked flying, and never been afraid in the air. So [.....**A**] felt very carefree as [.....**A**] boarded the plane with my mother at Lima. [.....**C**] was Christmas Eve. [.....**A**] were going to Pucallpa, up in the jungle, to join my father, and [.....**A**] knew [.....**C**] had prepared a Christmas tree to welcome [.....**A**].

12   The river which [.....**A**] had eventually found after so much agony was quite wide and had such a strong current that [.....**C**] often swept [.....**A**] off my feet. [.....**C**] just carried [.....**A**] along, and [.....**A**] knew how to swim. [.....**A**] had learnt well before 1967 when [.....**A**] went with my parents to live in the jungle.
    ['.....**B**] never know,' my father said at the time, '[.....**B**] never know if some day [.....**B**] might have to swim for your life in a river in the jungle.'

13   And then [.....**A**] heard voices from the forest. And [.....**A**] saw [.....**C**] coming. Three men in shorts and barefooted. [.....**A**] spoke Spanish with a strange accent. The [.....**C**] saw [.....**A**]. Ten and a half days after the crash that started [.....**C**] all, a human being talked to [.....**A**] again for the first time. 'Hey there,' [.....**C**] said. 'Who's sitting there?'

THE WRITE APPROACH

You are possibly going to face a survival situation one day. It's likely to arise out of something you do every day, such as travelling to school on the train or bus. It could arise out of some hobby or sport you engage in. Swimming is an obvious one, but others are bush walking, sailing, skiing and so on.

14 Select one of *your* every day situations or something *you* do as a sport or hobby. **THERE IS A DISASTER!** Write about how you survive it.

TALK TIME

15 Organise a debate on the topic: That survival is always just a matter of chance.

Don't forget that the passage offers evidence both *for* and *against* this statement.

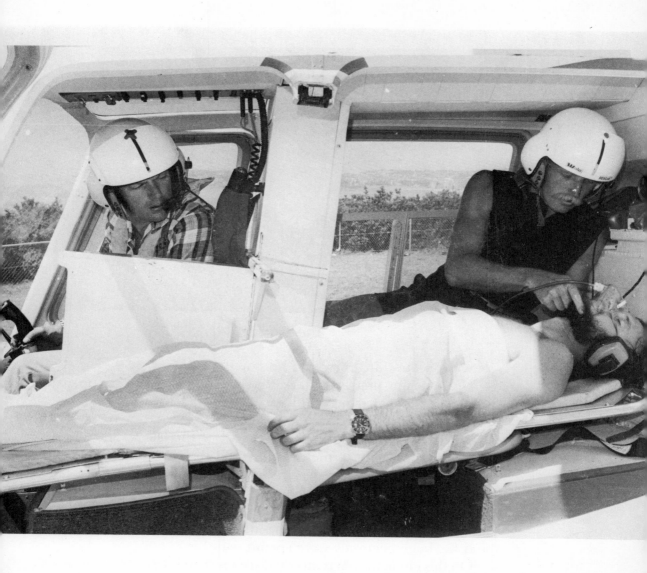

Unit Twelve: Fish

The big fish

It was on the third turn that he saw the fish first.

He saw him first as a dark shadow that took so long to pass under the boat that he could not believe its length.

'No,' he said. 'He can't be that big.'

But he was that big and at the end of this circle he came to the surface only thirty metres away and the man saw his tail out of water. It was higher than a big scythe blade and a very pale lavender above the dark blue water. It raked back and as the fish swam just below the surface the old man could see his huge bulk and the purple stripes that banded him. His dorsal fin was down and his huge pectorals were spread wide.

On this circle the old man could see the fish's eye and the two grey sucking fish that swam around him. Sometimes they attached themselves to him. Sometimes they darted off. Sometimes they would swim easily in his shadow. They were each over a metre long and when they swam fast they lashed their whole bodies like eels.

The old man was sweating now but from something else besides the sun. On each calm placid turn the fish made he was gaining line and he was sure that in two turns he would have a chance to get the harpoon in.

But I must get him close, close, close, he thought. I mustn't try for the head. I must get the heart.

'Be calm and strong, old man,' he said.

On the next circle the fish's back was out but he was a little too far from the boat. On the next circle he was still too far away but he was higher out of the water and the old man was sure that by gaining some more line he could have him alongside.

He had rigged his harpoon long before and its coil of light rope was in a round basket and the end was made fast to the bitt in the bow.

The fish was coming in on his circle now calm and beautiful-looking and only his great tail moving. The old man pulled on him all that he could to bring him closer. For just a moment the fish turned a little on his side. Then he straightened himself and began another circle.

'I moved him,' the old man said. 'I moved him then.'

He felt faint again now but he held on the great fish all the strain that he could. I moved him, he thought. Maybe this time I can get him over. Pull, hands, he thought. Hold up, legs. Last for me, head. Last for me. You never went. This time I'll pull him over.

But when he put all of his effort on, starting it well out before the fish came alongside and pulling with all his strength, the fish pulled part way over and then righted himself and swam away.

'Fish,' the old man said. 'Fish, you are going to have to die anyway. Do you have to kill me too?'

That way nothing is accomplished, he thought. His mouth was too dry to speak but he could not reach for the water now. I must get him alongside this time, he thought. I am not good for many more turns. Yes you are, he told himself. You're good for ever.

On the next turn, he nearly had him. But again the fish righted himself and swam slowly away.

You are killing me, fish, the old man thought. But you have a right to. Never have I seen a greater, or more beautiful, or a calmer or more noble thing than you, brother. Come on and kill me. I do not care who kills who.

Now you are getting confused in the head, he thought. You must keep your head clear. Keep your head clear and know how to suffer like a man. Or a fish, he thought.

'Clear up, head,' he said in a voice he could hardly hear. 'Clear up.'

Twice more it was the same on the turns.

I do not know, the old man thought. He had been on the point of feeling himself go each time. I do not know. But I will try it once more.

He tried it once more and he felt himself going when he turned the fish. The fish righted himself and swam off again slowly with the great tail weaving in the air.

I'll try it again, the old man promised, although his hands were mushy now and he could only see well in flashes.

He tried it again and it was the same. So, he thought, and he felt himself going before he started; I will try it once again.

He took all his pain and what was left of his strength and his long-gone pride and he put it against the fish's agony and the fish came over onto his side and swam gently on his side, his bill almost touching the planking of the skiff, and started to pass the boat, long, deep, wide, silver and barred with purple and interminable in the water.

The old man dropped the line and put his foot on it and lifted the harpoon as high as he could and drove it down with all his strength, and more strength he had just summoned, into the fish's side just behind the great chest fin that rose high in the air to the altitude of the man's chest. He felt the iron go in and he leaned on it and drove it further and then pushed all his weight after it.

Then the fish came alive, with his death in ·him, and rose high out of the water showing all his great length and width and all his power and his beauty. He seemed to hang in the air above the old man in the skiff. Then he fell into the water with a crash that sent spray over the old man and over all of the skiff.

The old man felt faint and sick and he could not see well. But he cleared the harpoon line and let it run slowly through his raw hands and, when he could see, he saw the fish was on his back with his silver belly up. The shaft of the harpoon was projecting at an angle from the fish's shoulder and the sea was discolouring with the red of the blood from his heart. First it was dark as a shoal in the blue water that was more than two kilometres deep. Then it spread like a cloud. The fish was silvery and still and floated with the waves.

The old man looked carefully in the glimpse of vision that he had. Then he took two turns of the harpoon line around the bitt in the bow and laid his head on his hands.

'Keep my head clear,' he said against the wood of the bow. 'I am a tired old man. But I have killed this fish which is my brother and now I must do the slave work.'

Now I must prepare the nooses and the rope to lash him alongside, he thought. Even if we were two and swamped her to load him and bailed her out, this skiff would never hold him. I must prepare everything, then bring him in and lash him well and step the mast and set sail for home.

ERNEST HEMINGWAY, *The Old Man and the Sea*

Dictionary

1 Before going on to answer the questions below, look up the following words in your back-of-the-book dictionary. Put them and their meanings side by side in your workbook.

(a) scythe   (b) dorsal
(c) raked   (d) pectorals
(e) skiff   (f) placid
(g) bitt   (h) accomplished
(i) interminable   (j) summoned

Check your understanding

2   Copy the frame and everything in it in your workbook. Write the answers to the following questions in the places provided in the frame.

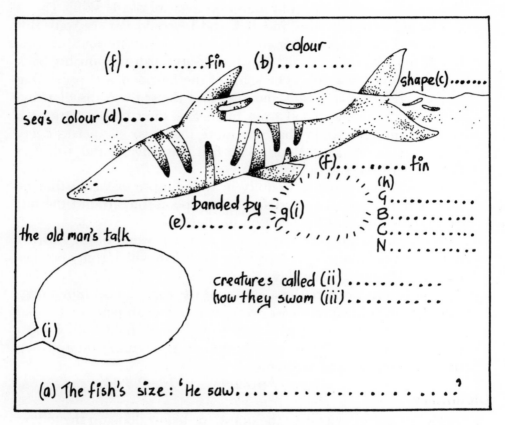

(f) . . . . fin   (b) . . . . colour

shape(c) . . . .

sea's colour (d) . . . . .

(f) . . . . fin

(h)
g . . . .
B . . . .
C . . . .
N . . . .

banded by ⌐g(i)
(e) . . . .

the old man's talk

creatures called (ii) . . . .
how they swam (iii) . . . .

(i)

(a) The fish's size: 'He saw. . . . .?'

(a)   Complete the description of the fish's size as seen by the old man.
(b)   What is the colour of the fish's tail?
(c)   What is the shape of the fish's tail?
(d)   What is the sea's colour?
(e)   The fish is banded by?
(f)   Where are his pectoral fins and dorsal fin? Which is which?

(g) (i) In the space provided draw the two other creatures that swim around the fish.
   (ii) Below the space put in what these other creatures are called.
   (iii) In words from the passage, describe *how* they swam.
(h) *G, B, C, N,* are the first letters of adjectives used by the old man to describe the fish. Complete the words.
(i) The old man not only talks to himself, he also talks to the fish. Put down the lines in which the old man talks directly to the fish and asks a question.

3 The fish 'rose high out of the water showing all his great length and width and all his power and his beauty'. What has happened just before this moment? (Write a couple of sentences.)

4 How does the old man feel after he harpoons the fish?

5 (a) What is the red blood from the fish's heart compared with when it is dark? Give the exact words from the passage.
   (b) Then it spread like [.....].

6 For 'slave work' as the old man calls it, he has to prepare 'the [n....] and [r....] to [.....], he thought.'

7 The two final things he has to do are concerned with the skiff. They are:
(a).....   (b).....

SPELLING

believe	surface	scythe	lavender
attached	pectorals	dorsal	placid
rigged	bitt	righted	accomplished
noble	mushy	agony	skiff
interminable	summoned	altitude	discolouring
silvery	glimpse	projecting	shoal

PRONOUN PUNCH UP!
VERBS TELL PRONOUNS TO TOE LINE OR ELSE!

These are the facts:

- Verbs are mostly **action** words. Right?
- Somebody or something has to perform the action. OK?
- Usually there's also somebody or something on the receiving end of the action. Right again?

Then, here's the punch line:

- The somebody or something that performs the action is called **the subject.** And, the somebody or something on the receiving end of the action is called **the object.**

In hard-hitting 'Old Man and the Sea' language it goes like this:

<u>The old man</u> harpoons <u>the fish</u>.

which becomes, when we use pronouns as stand-ins:

<u>He</u> harpoons <u>him</u>.

(The old man always calls the fish 'him')

Note how the *action of harpooning* forcibly links **subject** and **object.**

Now, as far as verbs are concerned, pronouns really have to toe the line. There are only certain pronouns that can act as the subject of an action, and only certain others that can act as the object. Here they all are jostling each other for your attention —

he   you   them   she   us   her   I   it   we   him   me   it
they   you

There's nothing new about them. You've come across them all before, standing in for male or female nouns, for this or that person, or for a number of people or things. As well as these jobs they also have to toe the line with verbs and act as their subjects or objects.

Most of the pronouns have different words for the subject and the object ['he' ..... 'him']. However, a couple of pronouns have the *same word* for both the subject and the object ['it' ..... 'it'].

Ladies and gentlemen, on my left we have **subjects** — on my right **objects**, with **action** in the middle of the ring.

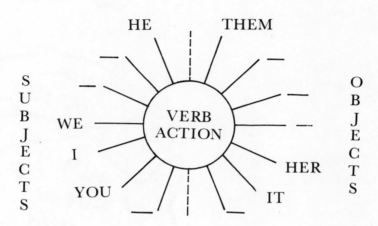

8 Copy this diagram in your workbook. Make the missing pronoun subjects and objects toe the line. Notice the follow-throughs from pronouns through verb action to the lines? Fill in the lines with the correct subjects and objects. Look back at the jostling pronouns to make sure you have used *all* the pronouns needed.

9 And now let's sail straight in amongst a shoal of sentences from the passage and haul in a catch of assorted pronouns used expertly as subjects and objects by Hemingway in *The Old Man and the Sea*.

● These sentences from the passage have been grouped in pairs, and for each pair you'll see a fish full of subject-object pronouns.

● Write out the sentences in your workbook and, as you go, add the pronouns.

● When you've finished, check your answers with the passage.

(a) [.....] saw [.....] first as a dark shadow that took so long to pass under the boat that [.....] could not believe its length.

(b) 'Fish, [.....] are going to have to die anyway. Do [.....] have to kill [.....] too?'

(c) [.....] are killing [.....], fish, the old man thought. This time [.....] 'll pull [.....] over.

(d) '[.....] moved [.....],' the old man said. '[.....] moved [.....] then.'

(e) On the next turn [.....] nearly had [.....].

(f) [.....] tried [.....] again and [.....] was the same.

(g) [.....] felt the iron go in and [.....] leaned on [.....] and drove [.....] further and then pushed all his weight after [.....].

(h) Even if [.....] were two and swamped [.....] to load [.....] and bailed [.....] out, this skiff would never hold [.....].

'Mighty Dog' from Carnation Co. Pty Ltd

PRONOUNS, LIKE DOGS, CAN GET VERY POSSESSIVE

What's a nice dog like Henry doing with all that money in his mouth?
Obviously he thinks it's *his!* Pronouns like 'mine' and 'his' can get very

possessive so, naturally, they are called **possessive pronouns**. And here they are:

mine   yours   theirs   his   hers   ours

10 (a) Copy these pronouns into your workbook.

(b) Put 1, 2, or 3 beside each pronoun according to whether it's a first, second or third person. (Remember, first person is the person speaking, second person is the person being spoken to, third person is the person or thing being spoken about.)

(c) Underline each pronoun with a single line if it is *singular* (standing in for one person or thing), or a double line if it is *plural* (standing in for more than one person or thing).

11 First take another long, hard look (that's hard cash he's got in his mouth) back at Henry.

The blank spaces represent nine missing possessive pronouns.

ours   mine   his   yours
yours   ours   mine   hers
theirs

Rearrange this list so that pronouns follow on in the order in which they would actually appear in the extract.

Henry

(Pant pant) as soon as I saw that bundle of lovely green and orange stuff lying on the footpath, I knew (pant pant) I had to have it. I had to make it [.....].

Well you wouldn't believe it, but I'd no sooner got my teeth round the lovely money when a big ugly hound of an Alsatian came galloping up.

'Hey!' he snarled, 'I've got a bone to pick with you! That money's not [.....], it's [.....]!'

Now, why should it be [.....]? I asked myself. So I growled as best I could through my mouthful of money, 'Listen here, mutt. You're barking up the wrong tree. OK? So be a good fella and go flap your ears elsewhere, will you?'

'Fella?' yelped the Alsatian. 'I'm no *fella*. I'm Annabelle.'

Wow! A *female*! (pant pant). Well, that was enough to make my tail wag like crazy. (Pant pant) I'm not greedy. The money needn't be [.....] or [.....], it can be [.....].

'OK!' yelped Annabelle excitedly as she took [.....].

So that's how Henry made the money [.....] rather than [.....].

And that's why he's grinning despite the fact that he's only holding half the mouthful he held before.

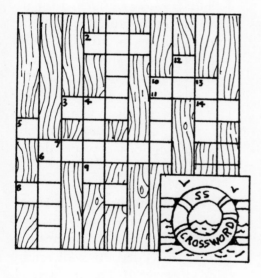

12 And now?
Let's relax for a moment.
Play a little deck quoits.

ACROSS

2 Can I give.....a lift?
3 The possessive form of 'it'.
6 Belonging to several people.
8 A first person, plural pronoun.
11 As 10 down, but standing in for a male.
14 [.....] is a boy.

DOWN

1 Belonging to you.
4 If the subject pronoun is 'they', the object pronoun is?
5 (diagonally) A simple little pronoun used for a thing, not a person.
7 'Them' is the object pronoun, '.....' is the subject pronoun
9 (diagonally) The object form of 'I'.
10 This is a possessive pronoun that stands in for a female.
12 (diagonally) 'And so say all of .....'
13 [.....] is a girl.

Unit Thirteen: Letter Writing

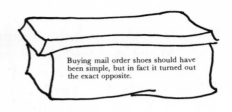

Buying mail order shoes should have been simple, but in fact it turned out the exact opposite.

Dear Shoe

Blooper Catalogues,
1880 Warehouse Street,
Chicago, Illinois. 60423.

Gentlemen,
I just received a pair of shoes ordered through your catalogue. They are the right colours . . . red toe, blue body, suede leather Oxfords. The right size and shape. And they go extremely well with my 100 per cent polyester knit bellbottom slacks which you sent earlier. But they are both left shoes. Left shoes. I would like one right shoe. Please advise.

Sincerely,
Robert Smythe

P.S. Note that it's Smythe with a 'y', not Smith with an 'i'.

Mr Robert Smythe,
18 Hicks Street,
Hayville, Ohio. 43500.

Dear Mr Smythe,
You say you received two left shoes from Blooper Catalogues. Well, that's impossible. These shoes are packed for us by the manufacturer, and he never makes a mistake. Will you try both shoes on again and see how wrong you are?

Yours truly,
Blooper Catalogues,
Hector Smurch,
Chief of Correspondence

Dear Mr Smurch,
Well, I tried them on again. I put the left shoe on my left foot and the other on my right foot, and proceeded to walk right into the wall. To prove it, I would send both shoes back. But I like these shoes. I might say I'm extremely fond of them. So I want to keep one left shoe and when I get the right shoe from you I'll have a pair of Oxfords that go so well with my slacks.

Yours truly,
Robert Smythe

Dear Mr Robert,
Mr Robert,
Mr Robert,
Your order has been received and your shoes will be delivered shortly. Blooper Catalogues thanks you for the order, the order, the order, and remember: When you want something super, order from Blooper.

Sincerely yours,
Blooper Catalogues

Dear Computer,
I did not order another pair of shoes. I simply wanted to know how to exchange a left shoe for a right shoe. I am sending by separate mail one of my two left shoes. Will you please replace it with a right shoe; same size, same colour and style?

Sincerely,
Robert Smythe

Dear Mr Sincerely,
Exchanges are not-not-not handled in this department. Your letter is being forwarded to our exchange department. And remember: By the pound or the bale, whatever you order, order by mail.

Blooper Catalogues

Dear Mr Smythe,
We do not exchange one shoe for another. In our entire history we have never had to do so. You are the first person who has ever had two left shoes delivered, if indeed that is the case. However, in order to keep your goodwill and still not admit any mistakes, we are sending you a pair of shoes exactly like the ones you ordered. Upon receipt of these, would you return your left shoe; that is, the remaining shoe, so that we can keep our inventory in order?

Sincerely,
M. Smith
P.S. You addressed your letter to 'Gentlemen'. I am not a gentleman. I am a woman. It's a common mistake in this man's world.

Dear Miss Smith,
Sorry about 'gentlemen', but how was I to know? Besides, it's standard business practice, which doesn't really reflect on anyone's gender. Anyhow, today I received TWO pairs of shoes from your company. One, sent by you. The other, by your computer. I now have

three left shoes and two right shoes and all I want is ONE pair of shoes to go with my 100 percent polyester knit bell-bottom slacks, and I'm beginning to lose my good humour about it. Please advise what I'm supposed to do now.

Annoyed,
Robert Smythe

Dear Mr Smythe,
Why don't you send all the shoes back, and we'll start all over again? I regret that you are annoyed. But I am annoyed, too. You've made another common male mistake. You addressed me as Miss Smith. You just assumed I was 'Miss'. If you should write again, will you please address me as Ms Smith . . . M-s Smith. Actually, I'm not married but I don't like people taking that for granted. And I prefer being called Ms Smith.

Yours truly,
Marge Smith

Dear Ms Smith,
I can't send all the shoes back. I'm now wearing a pair of them . . . the matching pair . . . a right shoe on my right foot and a left on the remaining foot. But I will return the second pair along with the extra left shoe as soon as I can get around to packing them. You see, I'm single, too, and in all my 27 years never learned to pack properly and I have no one to pack for me.

Cordially,
Bob Smythe

Dear Mr Shoe,
We have received your order for a right shoe, right shoe and Blooper Catalogues is pleased to send it to you, you, you.

Yours truly,
Smythe Catalogues

Dear Bob Smythe,
Why do you assume that if you were married your wife would have nothing to do but wrap your packages? It's time men did more around the house anyway. About the shoes, please return them promptly; that is, the remaining pair plus one, or our records will get all fouled up and I might lose the first job I've had since I got out of school two years ago.

Worried,
Marge Smith

Dear Marge,

I was about to return the remaining shoes when I received three right shoes in the mail . . . THREE. Somebody pushed the wrong button on the computer. I now have four right shoes and two left, not counting those I'm wearing with my 100 percent polyester bell-bottom slacks. If Blooper sends me any more shoes I can open a shoe store. See, I do have a sense of humour about it. Just to prove it, I will enclose a picture of me smiling. And I promise to forget all about the shoes if you send me a photo of you smiling. Or not smiling. Please forgive me for calling you by your first name but that's much more friendly than Ms Smith.

> Warmly,
> Bob

Dear Bob,

I don't mind your calling me Marge if that appeals to your masculine vanity. Incidentally, you have beautiful teeth, and features to match. Enclosed is a recent photograph of me. Please let me know what you think of it, or me, or both.

> Hurry,
> Marge

Dear Smythe,

Your complaint has just come to my attention. As head of this

organization I don't waste time. The way I understand it, you would like to have a pair of shoes that match. So, we're sending along such a pair. And you ordered a pair of slacks — 100 percent polyester bell-bottom slacks — to go with them. Right? OK, we'll throw these in on the house. Just don't bother us any more. Remember: Over land and over water, you'll always get your Blooper order.

Yours truly,
Horace Blooper

Dear 02348,
Your order has been forwarded to Horace Blooper, the president of Blooper Catalogues. You will next hear from him. Remember: Roses are red, violets are blue. Blooper Catalogues are right for you.

Sincerely,
Blooper Catalogues

Darling Marge,
Your picture blows my mind. I can't think of anything else, not even the extra shoes and free slacks. If you agree, I would like to meet you in Chicago. I'll leave as soon as you tell me where to meet you. I'll bring all the surplus shoes and deliver them to Mr Blooper in person.

Impatient,
Bob

Dear Bob,
I can't wait to see you. Meet me at the company office, second floor, front desk, as soon as you can make it. I'll have all the papers in order for the return of the shoes, so that the company books can be balanced.

Yours,
Marge

Sweet Marge,
If I promise to do my share in the kitchen and allow you to keep your identity by continuing to work, would you marry me? In Chicago? And people can throw rice and lots of shoes.

Love,
Bob

Wonderful Bob,
I can't believe it! It's fabulous. But just one little thing, Bob. When we meet in Chicago, how will I be able to recognize you?

Love,
Your future wife

My adorable Marge,

It will be quite easy to recognize me. I'll be wearing the same smile as in the photo . . . and my 100 percent knit polyester bell-bottom slacks, along with my two left shoes and carrying a large parcel.

> Love,
> Bob

MORT SINGER, *The Saturday Evening Post*

Check your understanding

The sequence of *Dear Shoe* letters illustrates a drastic — but humorous — communication breakdown between an individual, Robert Smythe, and an organization, Blooper Catalogues. See if you can get to the heart and soul (sole) of the matter by answering the following questions.

1 Find where the first sign of a misunderstanding creeps into the correspondence.

2 Bloopers assume something about their organization that is really too good to be true. What is their assumption?

3 In his third letter, Robert Smythe uses the greeting 'Dear Computer'. How does he know he has received a letter from a computer?

4 What amusing mistake in the form of greeting* does the computer make on 5 occasions? Quote these.

5 There is also quite a variation in the ending* too.
   (a) List these variations.
   (b) In which letter does the ending get confused with the greeting?

6 Write down all the commercial jingles that Bloopers manage to insert in their correspondence.

7 Robert Smythe gets into trouble over using 'miss' and 'gentlemen' in two of his letters.
   (a) Who objects?
   (b) What is the objection in each case?
   (c) What solution is proposed as far as the 'miss' is concerned?

*See **Letter Layouts** below.

 8　Robert Smythe confesses that he is unable to . . . What?
 9　His confession brings a women's rights response from Marge. What does she say?
10　Something begins to happen between Bob and Marge. What is it?
11　Mr Blooper himself writes — only to reveal that he, too, has misread the correspondence. What does he think Smythe needs?
12　(a)　What does Robert promise Marge?
　　(b)　In return for what?
13　Since the whole relationship between Marge and Robert has been by mail only, how will Marge recognize Robert when she meets him?

SPELLING

received	inventory	catalogue
truly	sincerely	addressed
manufacturer	addressee	business
correspondence	extremely	practice
computer	humour	separate
recognize	department	prefer
forwarded	organization	delivered
surplus		

LETTER LAYOUTS

There are several possible layouts for letters but they all have these features in common:
- the sender's address and postcode
- the date
- the addressee's name, address and postcode. (The addressee is the person to whom the letter is addressed — the person who receives the letter.)
- the greeting
- the body of the letter
- the ending
- the signature

Here is a typical letter layout showing where the above features usually go.

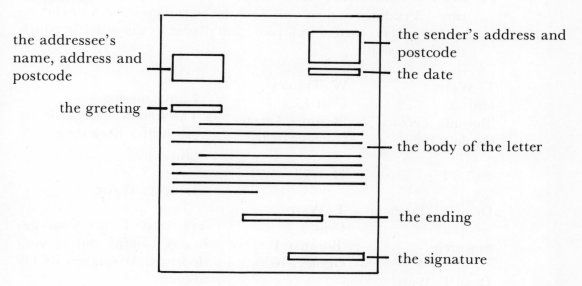

the addressee's name, address and postcode

the sender's address and postcode

the date

the greeting

the body of the letter

the ending

the signature

- Notice that the *Dear Shoe* letters omit the information on the sender. If they had put it in, they would have had to put it in on every letter. As it is, the first two letters in the Smythe-Blooper correspondence supply us with both the Blooper and Smythe addresses upper left.
- Notice that both the *Dear Shoe* letters and the typical letter above use what's called the **block** style. The other main style of letter layout is called **indent.** Here's the difference.

Block	**Indent**
Mr Robert Smythe	Mr Robert Smythe
18 Hicks Street,	18 Hicks Street,
Hayville, Ohio 43500.	Hayville, Ohio 43500.
Dear Mr Smythe,	Dear Mr Smythe,
See how all the lines are lined up on the left?	See how each line begins a space further in than the last?

Sorting out the features

14 Below are the mixed ingredients of 3 letters (3 greetings, 3 signatures, 3 endings and so on). Sort the features so that you end up with 3 letters, correct in layout, and placed in the order in which they were sent.

T. Watts
Unit 5,
'Boronia Terrace',
Gooley, 1026

10/1/77

Dear W. Tunney,

Sincerely,

Dear T. Watts,

9/1/77

W. Tunney

Sincerely,

TWatts

W. Tunney
Unit 13,
'Boronia Terrace',
Gooley, 1026

11/1/77

T. Watts
Unit 5,
'Boronia Terrace',
Gooley, 1026

I have no dog.
The sound you hear is my gas heater backfiring.

Sincerely,

Dear T. Watts,

Yesterday I met your gas heater coming out of your doorway. It wagged its tail at me!

Your barking dog is keeping me awake at night.
Please observe the rule that no pets are allowed in units.

Now bone up on a little sentence variety, as found in our correspondence.

"You're only going to the kennels for a week."

DIFFERENT SENTENCES — DIFFERENT PURPOSES

We use different kinds of sentences for different purposes.

- To state the facts: This room is a mess. (**statement)**
- To exclaim: What a mix-up! (**exclamation** — with an exclamation mark)
- To give an order: Get this place tidied up. (**order** or **command**)
- To request: Please see if you can put a few things away. (**request**)
- To ask a question: Why don't you put things away? (**question** — with a question mark)
- To express a wish: It would be good if everything was in its place. (**wish**)

15 Find 3 examples of each of these kinds of sentence in the *Dear Shoe* correspondence.
- (a)   statement
- (b)   exclamation
- (c)   order or command
- (d)   question
- (e)   request
- (f)   wish

16 Try your hand at putting in the commas, full stops and capitals in this letter.

> 16 lavender blue st
> heart throb sydney
> nsw 2050
> 20th november 1977

ms juliette wonderful
19 rainbow crescent
primrose sydney nsw 2030

dear ms wonderful

> i picked up the tissue you dropped and i will cherish it till i hear from you

> yours hopefully
> bob romeo

Feeling confident enough to write — and receive — a few letters of your own?

Here we go then.

"Personally, I think he's getting too confident."

DEAR SHOE YOURSELF!

17 This is just between your neighbour and yourself. In this exercise, the two of you are asked to write letters to each other.

- Look at the columns below. There's a sender's column, an addressee's column, and a kind of letter column.

- Here's all you do. Both of you choose a sender, different ones of course.

- As soon as you've chosen a sender, look across at the addressee's column to see whom you're writing to. For example, the patient writes to the dentist.

- Now choose the kind of letter you're going to write from the kind of letter column. For example, the patient writes a complaining letter to the dentist. *You* decide what goes in the letter. (Maybe all your fillings have just crumbled away!)

- Take care to use the correct layout and punctuation pattern.

- As soon as you and your neighbour have both finished your letters — exchange them. For example, while *you* have decided to be a patient writing to your dentist (your neighbour), *your neighbour* may have decided to be a housewife writing to her greengrocer (you). This means you each *write* and *receive* a letter.

- Now each of you writes a suitable reply to the letter you've received.
- Exchange your replies.

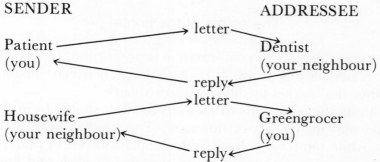

SENDER   ADDRESSEE

Patient (you) → letter → Dentist (your neighbour)
Dentist → reply → Patient (you)

Housewife (your neighbour) → letter → Greengrocer (you)
Greengrocer → reply → Housewife (your neighbour)

Correspondence masterpieces should be read out to the rest of the class!

	SENDER	ADDRESSEE	LETTER
(a)	Patient	Dentist	Complaining letter
(b)	Housewife	Greengrocer	Letter giving information
(c)	Garbage inspector	Householder	Letter of praise or congratulations
(d)	Policeman	Law breaker	
(e)	Teacher	Student's parents	
(f)	Landlord	Tenant	

Feel free to add other interesting senders, addressees and kinds of letters that *you* think up.

"YOU WANT ALL THESE SENT AIR MAIL. RIGHT?"

Unit Fourteen: Horse

The points of the horse

The great thing about conformation is proportion. In any creature that is perfect physically, it is the balance between one part and another that makes for beauty and strength.

This applies especially to a horse's **head**. It should be in absolute proportion to the rest of the body. Too small a head looks just silly, while too large a head looks, and is, heavy. A large, heavy head means a continual drag on the horse's neck and forehead, and causes it to tire sooner. It is in the head that breeding, or lack of it, shows most clearly. The diagram shows some of the points which follow.

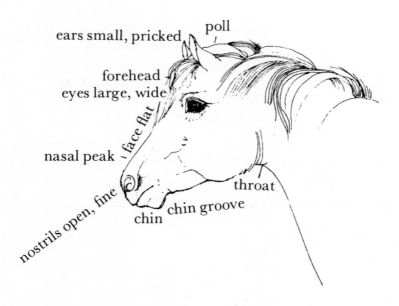

A well-bred head should look lean, almost bony, the lines of the jaw and *cheek bones* clean and finely drawn. The points to look for are width between the eyes, depth through the jaw, softness of *muzzle*, wide-open, fine *nostrils*. You can always tell the velvety sensitive lips of a breedy horse from the thick coarse ones of a commoner; from a pony to a Percheron this holds good. The **eyes** should be large and wide, and should have a keen and friendly expression. They should stand well out, so that they can see all round; their owner is then not apt to be nervous or suspicious. Small, deep-set eyes usually show an unreliable disposition; and, generally, you should avoid a horse that is always showing the whites of its eyes.

The **face** of a good horse is usually flat or slightly concave. This is seen mostly in thoroughbreds and, in the extreme, in Arabs, and is called being stag- or dish-faced. The opposite, when the line of the face is convex, is called Roman-nosed. This is not necessarily a sign of bad breeding unless the head is also out of proportion; many heavy breeds, the cold-blooded strains, cart-horses, and the like, are inclined to be Roman-nosed, and none the worse for that. The great thing is for the line of the face and **forehead** to be smooth. The horse to avoid is one with a lump between its eyes. Nobody has explained its effect but all I know is that, personally, I have never met a horse like this which had not got some sort of kink which made it unreliable, and often dangerous.

The **ears** should be fairly small and well pricked, that is, habitually carried forward, with an air of intelligent interest in what lies ahead. However, big ears and lop-ears, though popularly supposed to denote sluggishness and technically a fault in the show ring, do not, so far as I can see, affect performance at all. But you should study a horse's ears carefully: they are a sort of barometer to tell you what the equine weather is going to be: pricked forward — set fair; moving backwards and forwards — change; laid back — look out for squalls.

Your **position** on a horse should be firm and as easy as possible for the horse.

The typical modern English position is not one into which you will fall naturally. Most beginners, if left to themselves, will sit back too far towards the cantle of the saddle, while some beginners manage to get themselves into a far-forward position, which is the Italian forward seat gone entirely wrong.

There are a number of points to remember about the correct position.

(1) There is a general impression of alertness without stiffness. (2) The rider is in the lowest part of the saddle. (3) There is a space of at least a hand's breadth between his seat and the cantle. (4) The head is up, eyes looking to the front and not downwards — the line of sight is between the horse's ears. (5) The shoulders are square. (6) The chest is normal. (7) The back is hollowed, but not in an exaggerated way. (8) The waist is supple — there is nothing slouching or round-shouldered about the upper part of the body. (9) The seat and legs are close to the horse without undue pressure. (10) The thighs, knees, and calves tend to turn inwards. (11) The leg below the knee slopes back so that the heels are behind the girth, roughly in the same vertical line as the seat bones. (12) The heels are pressed down with the ankles bent so that the toes are pointing up and slightly outwards. (13) The weight is taken on the stirrup irons by the ball of the foot. (14) The hand is held in the conventional military position, elbows close to the sides. (15) The elbow, forearm, wrist, hand, and rein are in one straight line to the bit. The hands should not be held too close together.

It requires practice and perseverance to acquire this position, but when your muscles have been developed and organized for it, you will find it really firm and practical and, most important, it allows your horse full play for all the muscles of movement and balance.

The great aim is to attain a firm and independent seat, independent, that is, of the reins, which are not meant for hanging on with, and to some extent independent of the stirrups. If you have an independent seat, you have gone a long way towards having good hands.

C. E. G. HOPE, Riding

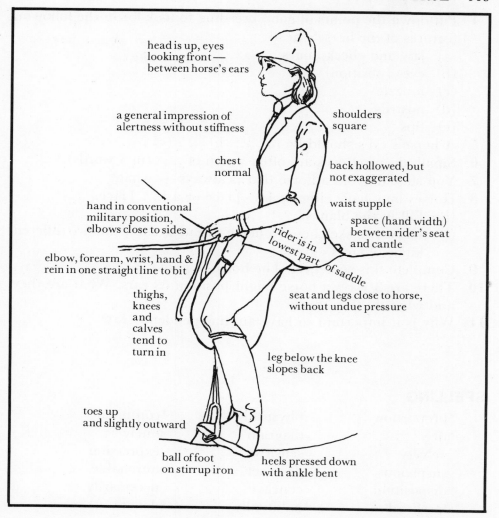

head is up, eyes looking front — between horse's ears

a general impression of alertness without stiffness

shoulders square

chest normal

back hollowed, but not exaggerated

hand in conventional military position, elbows close to sides

waist supple

space (hand width) between rider's seat and cantle

rider is in lowest part of saddle

elbow, forearm, wrist, hand & rein in one straight line to bit

thighs, knees and calves tend to turn in

seat and legs close to horse, without undue pressure

leg below the knee slopes back

toes up and slightly outward

ball of foot on stirrup iron

heels pressed down with ankle bent

Check your understanding

1 What is it that makes for beauty and strength in any creature?
2 What is wrong with a horse having a small head?
3 A large head is a more serious matter. Why?

4   Put down the points of good breeding to look for in the following features of the horse's head:
   (a) jaw and cheek bones
   (b) eyes (position)
   (c) muzzle
   (d) nostrils
   (e) lips

5   A horse's eyes should be (a)..... (b) ..... (c) .....

6   Small, deep-set eyes are often a sign of ..... (in 3 words).

7   You should avoid a horse that is always — what?

8   Horses may have either a [.....] face or a [....] face.
   (a) Fill in the blanks.
   (b) Draw two sketches of a horse's head to show the two different kinds of faces.

9   Complete this sentence: 'The horse to avoid .....'

10   There are 3 ways a horse might position its ears. What are they, and what do they mean?

11   Why is it important to have an 'independent' seat?

SPELLING

*proportion	physically	*continual
*tire	diagram	finely
velvety	sensitive	expression
suspicious	deep-set	unreliable
*disposition	concave	necessarily
forehead	*habitually	*denote
*affect	performance	barometer
squalls	junction	looseness
inclined	*effect	personally

12   An asterisk (*) indicates words you may not know the meanings of. Look them up in the dictionary at the back of the book, and then put both words and meanings down side by side in your workbook.

THE WIZARD OF ID —   **By Parker and Hart**

SADDLE UP AND RIDE OFF SLOWLY INTO THE
SENSIBLE WORLD OF SENTENCES

You dream up a horse. You see it in your mind's eye. You go to put it down on paper — and realize you're back with all the good old familiar parts of speech and punctuation marks. Let's round them up and see what we've got.

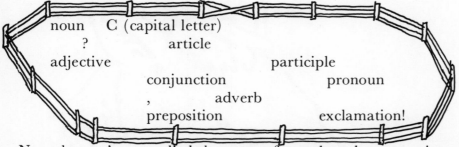

noun   C (capital letter)
    ?   article
adjective   participle
        conjunction   pronoun
        ,   adverb
        preposition   exclamation!

Now that we've corralled the parts of speech and punctuation marks, we can go ahead and rope in this one or that to form your dreamed up horse into a sentence on paper.

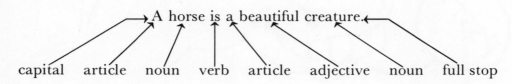

A horse is a beautiful creature.

capital   article   noun   verb   article   adjective   noun   full stop

13   Now rope in whatever parts of speech and punctuation marks you need for the following thoughts—sentences on paper.
- Write out the sentences, correcting punctuation as you go.
- Below each sentence put in the part of speech for each word, and the punctuation marks.

Line them up!

(a) A good horse usually has a flat or slightly concave face.

(b) a noble head looks lean and almost bony

(c) small deep-set eyes show an unreliable disposition

(d) are the eyes large and wide

(e) good ears are fairly small but alert

(f) on a horse a lump between the eyes means bad trouble

SUBJECT AND PREDICATE

This man gets it straight from the horse's mouth. And straight from the horse's mouth the whisper is that every good (one-thought) sentence has a **subject** and a **predicate**.

The subject is what the sentence is all about,

This man

while the predicate supplies the verb and all the rest.

gets it straight from the horse's mouth.

Subject and predicate together give

This man gets it straight from the horse's mouth.

Why should anyone *care* whether a sentence has both a subject *and* a predicate? The answer is that a good sentence is like a good horse, complete in itself. A good sentence should express (bring out) a single complete thought. In order to express a complete thought, a sentence must have a subject and a predicate, and the *verb* is an important part of the predicate.

14 Now let's mount an exercise in which you shuffle round a few subjects and predicates. Here are 5 sentences from the passage in which subjects have been separated from predicates.
- Put them back together again so that they make sense.
- When you're finished check your answers out in the passage.

	SUBJECTS	PREDICATES
(a)	The rider	is not one into which you would fall naturally.
(b)	The hands	is in the lowest part of the saddle.
(c)	The shoulders	are in one straight line to the bit.
(d)	The typical modern English position	should not be held too close together.
(e)	The elbow, forearm, wrist, hand, and rein	are square.

OVERLAPPING SENTENCES

Reminder, **one sentence** equals **one complete thought.** Here's a sentence that is overlapping drastically:

> A good rider puts the horse first and when a long ride is finished the horse is fed and watered before the rider has a meal and bath so that the horse always comes first and that's the way to keep your horse a happy and a healthy animal!

What a mouthful! You can't even say it in one breath. Most good sentences can be said in one comfortable breath. If you want to write longer sentences, put in commas where one would normally pause to take another breath.

However, commas are not going to cure the fearsome disease of overlap that the above 'sentence' is suffering from. No, there are just too many thoughts overlapping each other. Notice how they are artificially held together by conjunctions (and, so). What we have to do is to *separate* the *distinct thoughts* into sentences of their own.

> A good rider puts the horse first. When a long ride is finished, the horse is fed and watered before the rider has a meal and a bath. The horse always comes first. That's the way to keep your horse a happy and healthy animal!

15 Now try doing a similar rewrite job on the following overlapping sentences. Your aim is to produce sentences with distinct and separate thoughts of their own.

   (a) The rider in the picture has her shoulders squared and her legs below the knees slope back and her toes are pointed upwards in the stirrups.

   (b) The picture shows that she has a firm grip on the reins it looks great.

   (c) A slumped position does not allow you to guide your horse properly so it is always better to keep your head up with your eyes looking to the front between the horse's ears this is also a much more comfortable position to take up.

USE SHORT SHORT SENTENCES AND THE LAUGH'S ON YOU!

Avoid this kind of thing:

> My horse is called Sally. She gallops well. She also stops suddenly. This is a bad habit.

A build-up of short short sentences can be just as boring as the long, overlapping kind. This reads and sounds much better:

> My horse is called Sally. Although she gallops well, she has a bad habit of stopping suddenly.

Notice that by using 'although' and by cutting down and combining short sentences we have given ourselves a smoother ride. Things flow along rather than jerk along. We can also use other words such as 'when', 'where', 'because' to begin sentences that will give us a smoother ride.

16 The three groups of short short sentences below can each be combined into one sentence by using 'when', 'where' or 'because' to begin them. Write the smoother ride sentences in your workbook.
(a) A horse must be mounted properly. You should use a springy step. You spring off the right foot. [when]
(b) A horse is a sensitive animal. Your movements should be slow and natural. Avoid making sudden or violent movements. [because]
(c) The possibility of danger must be avoided. You must rein in your horse. Rein in to a walk. [where]

WELL GROOMED SENTENCES

Like well groomed horses, well groomed sentences need a lot of tender loving care (TLC).

TLC means giving that little extra something to nouns, seeing that verbs get a little more action, adding a phrase here or there, and so on. Let's take that first sentence again.

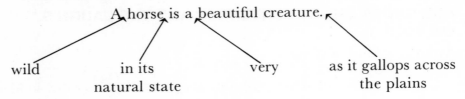

A wild horse in its natural state is a very beautiful creature as it gallops across the plains.

17   Try your hand at smoothly grooming these sentences.
   (a)   I would like to own a pony.
   (b)   The big mare is angry.
   (c)   Some horses are easily trained.
   (d)   Most horses love sugar.
   (e)   Saddles cost a lot.

THE WRITE APPROACH

18   The topic is 'The day I tamed a wild horse'. But there's *one* condition. You must begin each sentence in a different way. Begin with an adverb, an article plus noun, an article plus adjective plus noun, a preposition plus phrase, a pronoun, a participle, etc. The order does not matter, but variety does!

TALK TIME

Think about it . . . 'animals can teach *us* a lot'.
   On the surface, it doesn't *seem* very likely but . . . the more you think about it the more you can find in its favour.

19   Take five minutes to jot down a few points in favour of the idea of humans learning from animals. Then try persuading the rest of the class — if they need persuading — that animals *can* teach us a lot.

Unit Fifteen: Teenager

Teenager care

THE PARENTS' PART

Congratulations! You are now the proud parent of a brand new teenager. The child you once weaned, coddled and pampered is no more. He now stands on the threshold of adulthood. And in the next seven years (13-19) he may even *reach* adulthood. Then again, it may take him until he's 30.

When you take your first good look at him, you may be shocked. He will probably be very hairy, have skin blemishes, and dress like a hobo. And he might remain in this condition throughout his teens. Or, he might become *ugly!* In any case, don't worry.

You will probably receive all kinds of advice on how to care for your brand new teenager. You may even feel that obeying your first natural impulse is the best. Don't do it!

Obey your second natural impulse. Care for him, show him you love him and want him, and try to accept him as best as you can. But above all, ignore that first natural impulse! Strangulation is still punishable by death in some States!

The problem of health. This is an area that always concerns the parents of a new teenager. But with medical science making such great strides of late, this is a needless worry. If you follow the doctor's instructions carefully, you may very well live to be 40.

The main concern of the father. While the mother will bear the initial brunt of caring for a teenager, the father must not be forgotten. His primary problem will be that of jealousy. For the first time, his wife will be dividing her affection between two people: a big, self-sufficient figure, and a small, helpless creature. As a small, helpless creature, the father resents this.

CLOTHING AND EQUIPMENT

A teenager's clothing and equipment are very important. Here is a partial list of the things your new teenager will need:

Eight pairs of dirty sneakers.

Seventeen baggy sweatshirts.

One hundred and seven pairs of blue jeans.

Two leather motorcycle jackets.

One Nazi officer's cap.

One athletic supporter.

(Note: Also see Section 38 — Clothing for the Teenage Boy.)

CARING FOR YOUR TEENAGER

Feeding him. Eating habits vary according to the size and weight of the teenager. But ordinarily, here is a good daily feeding schedule to follow:

8:00 a.m., 10:00 a.m., Noon, 3:00 p.m., 3:45 p.m., 6:00 p.m., 7:00 p.m., 7:30 p.m., 8:15 p.m., 9:30 p.m., 10:00 p.m., 11:00 p.m., 11:30 p.m., Midnight, 2:00 a.m.

(Note: This is the regular feeding schedule. Between meals feeding should be arranged at your discretion.)

Mixing the daily formula. This is a relatively simple procedure. Merely mould 52 hamburgers into patties, add seasoning, and serve periodically throughout the day and night with Coke and pizza. If the teenager is not crying too loudly for his food, you might even try to *cook* the hamburgers first from time to time.

BATHING AND GROOMING

Bathing and grooming of a teenager is always of prime importance to a parent. The following are all the tips, advice and tricks that have proved effective in the past for guiding the teenager in the art of proper bathing and grooming:

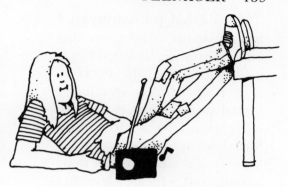

PLAYTIME

One of his favourite games is Hanging Around. This consists of sitting around the house (on anything but a chair) in a way that his feet are always higher than his head, with a completely vacant expression on his face, and saying and doing absolutely nothing. A teenager can play this game for days, often years.

Sometimes this game frightens parents, because they don't know if the teenager is alive or not. Remember this: taking his pulse is a waste of time. In this condition, he has a way of making his pulse stop, too. You will know when your teenager is really dead by the intelligent look on his face.

Disciplining the teenager. From time to time, you will find it necessary to discipline your teenager. There are three methods of punishment which I suggest you can try:

(a) **Deprive him of something.** This is a very tricky punishment because a teenager usually has everything. And even if you take something away from him, he can usually replace it on his own. So the thing to do is to deprive him of something he doesn't want in the first place. For example, say to him, 'Just for that you can't play pinochle next Tuesday!' Chances are he doesn't even know what pinochle *is*, but the bizarre nature of what you have said will make him do a lot of thinking . . . which for most teenagers is punishment in itself.

(b) **Verbal punishment.** I usually do not advocate yelling and screaming, but at times it does help to clear the air. Here is the proper way to administer verbal punishment to a teenager: Stand on a chair, look him straight in the eye, and tell him sternly what he has done wrong, and why he shouldn't do it again. The more you holler at him and threaten him, the more frightened he will become . . . that he might kill you.

(c) **Physical punishment.** Laying hands on a teenager should only be done as a last resort. It can sometimes be very dangerous for you. (See preceding paragraph.) In any case, remember this: Never strike a teenager while you are angry. Wait until your anger at him has cooled off. This may not happen until he is 73, at which time you might consider ramming his wheelchair with yours and letting it go at that.

BEHAVIOUR PROBLEMS

Temper tantrums. Teenagers are usually jumpy and high-strung. They become very emotional at strange times and for no apparent reasons. For example, when asked to take out the garbage, a teenager may giggle hysterically, then begin to scream, and wind up crying bitterly. There is a simple explanation for this: the teenager *identifies* with garbage.

The wisest thing to do is to let most tantrums run their course. However, if a tantrum persists, I recommend a good pacifier. (See your local Sports Car Dealer in the Yellow Pages.)

CONCLUSION

It takes time to get used to a new teenager. Be patient with him and, above all, show him all the love you can. But, by all means, do not worry or feel guilty if you cannot actually love him. Your lack of love in the beginning is a temporary condition which seldom lasts for more than the seven years he is a teenager. (For what to do then, read my next book, *Oh, My God, He's Twenty!*)

LARRY SIEGEL *Mad Special*

Check your understanding

The questions, of course, warily circle the teenager.

10 When does a teenager really look intelligent?

9 There's something a teenager can do for days — even years. What is it?

8 Give a reason for leaving the blank space below bathing and grooming.

7 Notice how the humour in the passage is dangled like a fish hook? Bait: you read about the preparation of the hamburgers . . . Hook: right at the end comes the information that they are not even . . . (What?)

6 What is unusual about the feeding schedule outlined in the passage? Say what you think a teenager might consume at midnight.

5 Quite apart from the list of clothing and equipment given, there's no doubt *you* will be able to supply items and quantities of gear that *you* think are essential.

So, go ahead and jot down a quick list of your own.

Is it for the teenage girl, boy, or both?

1 When you take your first look at your new teenager you may be shocked. Why? Give 3 reasons.

2 What is the first natural impulse you might have towards your new teenager?

3 The problem of health . . . for whom is it a problem?

4 The teenager is [b.....] and [s.....] while the father is [s.....] and [h.....]. (Supply the missing words.)

SPELLING

congratulations	*brunt	*effective	*apparent
adulthood	affection	*partial	*identifies
*impulse	*self-sufficient	schedule	persist
instructions	*resents	*discretion	recommend
*initial	*prime	*periodically	*pacifier
*deprive	conclusion	*bizarre	

11 The asterisked words appear in the back-of-the-book dictionary. Look them up, and write them with their meanings in your workbook.

PARAGRAPHS!

Run your eye over *Teenage Care*. All the rectangles of print are paragraphs.

- Paragraphs vary a lot in size. Some are long, some short. It's even possible to have a *one line* paragraph!
- The first line of each paragraph is *indented* (pushed or dented in). Indent and it's much easier to see where each new paragraph begins. (Sometimes you will find that, as in this book, a paragraph is not indented if it is the first paragraph in a section.)

How do you find out what the topic is?

Long or short, all paragraphs have one thing in common: there's *one* idea or **topic** per paragraph, and one *only*!

There's usually one sentence in any paragraph that lays the topic right on the line for you! Often the topic glares out at you from the first sentence. The sentence that holds up this placard for you is naturally called **the topic sentence.** In *Teenager Care*, bold black printing is used to direct the reader's attention to either a topic sentence or heading.

Now look back at the first paragraph of *Teenager Care*. It's made up of the topic sentence, indicating the topic itself, and four other sentences. Let's stretch things a little by putting down the topic sentence and then going from sentence to sentence in turn to show how each expands on the topic.

Congratulations! You are now the proud parent of a brand new teenager.

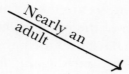

The child you once weaned, coddled and pampered is no more.

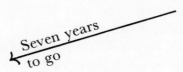

He now stands on the threshold of adulthood.

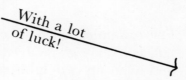

And in the next seven years (13-19) he may even reach adulthood.

Then again it may take him until he's 30.

Notice how every sentence expands on, or adds a little more to, the topic?

12 Take the second paragraph and stretch *it* a little.
  (a) Put down the topic sentence.
  (b) Plant a little placard displaying the topic in a few brief words.
  (c) Space out the other sentences in the paragraph and link them to the topic sentence with arrows.
  (d) Write a few words along the arrows to show how each sentence in turn expands on the topic.

Sense and sentences

Sentences in a paragraph should follow on from each other so that the whole paragraph makes sense.

13 The following paragraphs are taken from *Teenager Care*. However, the sentences in each of the paragraphs have been mixed around a little. Put the sense back into the paragraphs by rearranging the sentences so that they, once again, follow on from each other correctly. Check by looking at the passage.

  (a) • If you follow the doctor's instructions carefully, you may very well live to be 40.
       • The problem of health.
       • But with medical science making such great strides of late, this is a needless worry.
       • This is an area that always concerns the parents of a new teenager.

  (b) • For example, when asked to take out the garbage, a teenager may giggle hysterically, then begin to scream, and wind up crying bitterly.
       • Teenagers are usually jumpy and high-strung.
       • There is a simple explanation for this: the teenager identifies with garbage.
       • They become very emotional at strange times and for no apparent reasons.

(c)
- So the thing to do is to deprive him of something he doesn't want in the first place.
- Deprive him of something.
- And even if you take something away from him, he can usually replace it on his own.
- This is a very tricky punishment because a teenager usually has everything.
- Chances are he doesn't know what pinochle is, but the bizarre nature of what you have said will make him do a lot of thinking...which for most teenagers is punishment in itself.
- For example, say to him, 'Just for that you can't play pinochle next Tuesday!'

PARAGRAPHING SPEECH

How do you paragraph speech? Look at this example:

Once bitten

'Hi, Jane.'

'Hi, Bob.'

'Er, Jane . . .'

'Yes, Bob?'

'Er, well,' Bob stammered, 'I rushed out this morning without grabbing my lunch and I was wondering . . .'

'You mean you'd like one of my sandwiches?' Jane asked.

Bob nodded and Jane offered the packet.

'Help yourself.'

Bob grabbed a sandwich and bit into it. He chewed, gulped and gasped.

'*What* was in *that*?'

'Shredded onion weed spiced with underdone chili and garnished with green oodle nuts. Have another one.'

Bob shook his head. 'Er, no thanks. Not just at the moment.' He hurried away.

'Pity,' sighed Jane, 'there goes another possible friendship down the drain. Oh, well,' she mumbled as she bit into a sandwich and chewed contentedly, 'you can't win 'em all.'

- Each new item of speech is given a new line of its own. It becomes a one-line paragraph, a two-line paragraph, or whatever length the speech runs to.
- If a speaker simply continues after a break in speech (*sighed Jane*, or *Bob stammered*), do not begin a new line. The speech simply carries on after the break. Do not use a capital letter, unless you begin a new sentence.
- Each line that begins a paragraph needs to be indented.

THE WRITE APPROACH

14 This is a creative writing exercise with the title 'The Hungry Teenager'. You're given 4 topic sentences with which to begin 4 paragraphs.

- Write out the topic sentences and complete the paragraphs, using your imagination.
- Make sure that each paragraph flows smoothly on to the topic sentence that follows.

TOPIC SENTENCES

(a) All the way home I felt ravenous so, as soon as I got in, I went straight to the fridge . . .

(b) An hour later I suddenly realized what I'd done . . .

(c) Mum was very upset . . .

(d) The punishment seemed unfair and I argued about it, but as usual it was useless . . .

TALK TIME

15 Teenagers talk back . . .

Each class member prepares a one-minute talk on things that make teenagers **special**, or **different**, or **unique**, or just downright **awful**!

Use the passage to help your ideas along.

SQUEEZE A WORD

16 See how many words you can squeeze out of 'ADOLESCENT' ('cent' is an obvious one.)

Compete with your neighbour by setting a time limit of 5 minutes. See who has the most words when the time's up!

17 When you've finished, try 'TEENAGERS'.

18 Now, let's go a step further. Copy down this sentence: 'ONE OF HIS FAVOURITE GAMES IS HANGING AROUND.'

Here the aim, once again, is to squeeze out as many concealed words from the sentence as you can. Set yourselves a time limit of 5 minutes. One catch: you must form your words from the letters of the sentence in the *same order* as they occur in the sentence. For example, 'on', 'no' . . . get the idea?

When you've finished, choose another sentence from *Teenage Care*, and try squeezing that too!

Unit Sixteen: Bushfire

Tips to safeguard you and your home

Fires have already blackened wide tracts of Australian bushland this summer, and the risk of further outbreaks is high.

'The season got off to a bad start,' said a spokesman for the NSW State Emergency Services. 'We've had a wet year with a lot of growth. Now that growth is starting to die back and act as fuel.

'Hot weather, low humidity and strong winds are about the worst possible combination of conditions we could get. It could be a very bad season indeed.'

The following precautions are suggested by the NSW Bush Fire Council:

- Don't leave branches overhanging the house.
- Clean out leaves from gutters.
- Fit gauze to windows and ventilators.
- Box in open eaves.
- Clear away dry timber and rubbish.
- Clear undergrowth from fences.
- Burn off long grass at safe times.
- Store inflammable liquids away from the house and well out of the reach of fire.

If there are fires in your area, shut all windows and doors. Most house fires are started under or inside the roof by flying sparks, so keep a ladder close to a manhole in your ceiling.

Block downpipes with tennis balls and fill your guttering with water. Have your garden hoses connected, and make sure they reach beyond boundary fences.

Should fire race towards your home *don't* put furniture out in the street. That's where much furniture is destroyed during bushfires.

You are not covered by insurance if your furniture is outside.

Wear long-sleeved cotton shirts or blouses, jeans and a floppy hat. Put on stout shoes and avoid nylon clothing.

If fire is very close and you are in a car don't try to outrun the flames. Lie down on the floor of the car with all the windows and doors closed, and preferably with a blanket or coat covering you.

A roaring blaze will take 90 seconds to pass, and your chances of survival in the great heat are much better inside the car. Don't worry, the chance of the petrol tank exploding is almost nil.

Should your children be at school during an outbreak of fire, that is probably the safest spot for them. The school-yard forms a natural fire break.

Even when the fire has passed it is wise to check ceilings for flying embers often during the next few hours. Buckets should be full of water during this time.

Finally, if you are not in a danger area stay away from fire-fighting areas unless you plan to help. Sightseers are a hazard.

SEAN MOYLAN, *The Australian Women's Weekly*

Check your understanding

1 Copy the following crossword into your workbook and answer the questions.

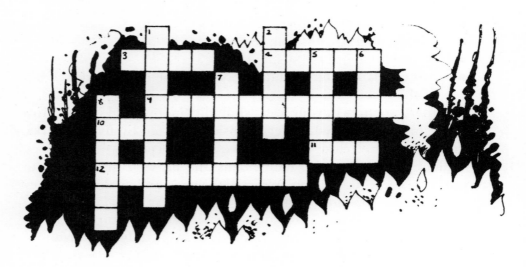

ACROSS

3 What dead vegetation is for a fire.

4 The act of deliberately lighting a fire, to cause harm.

9 Such liquids should be stored well away from the house.

10 Something that *is* welcome by those fighting fires.

11 The schoolyard is a safe place for the younger . . .

12 Should be filled with water if there are fires in the area.

DOWN

1 When this is low, conditions for bushfires are worse.

2 Country properties often hit hard by bush fires.

5 Most house fires are caused by one of these catching inside the roof.

6 Your 'almost chance' of a car petrol tank exploding in a

7 fire.
Where to lie if trapped in your car by a fire.

8 Only helpers are wanted at a fire if they are from outside this area.

WORKING WITH PREPOSITIONS

Prepositions are best understood by looking at the meaning of their name. 'Pre' is a syllable which begins many words, and means 'before'. 'Position' means 'placed'. A preposition is basically a word that is placed before another word.

What other word does a preposition come before? Prepositions have been given their name because they are almost always positioned before a noun (or pronoun). This noun (or pronoun) is usually referred to as the **object** of the preposition.

Preposition	Preposition	Preposition
Noun	Noun	Noun
in the boat	over the fence	with me

There are exceptions to this pattern, but they do not occur very often. The most common exception occurs when a sentence ends with a preposition, so that no other word follows the preposition.

It was something he would not put up with.

What does a preposition do?

- **Prepositions start phrases.** A phrase is a group of words that goes together but does not contain a verb with a subject.

  inside the roof

- **Prepositions link words.** Though they are small usually, prepositions do important work in linking words together so that we understand their relationship with each other.

  Clear undergrowth from fences.

The preposition 'from' links 'undergrowth' and 'fences' in such a way that we understand where the undergrowth should be cleared. 'Fences' is the object of 'from'. Leave out the preposition, and the relationship is no longer clear.

  Clear undergrowth fences.

Commonly used prepositions

off	into	down
in	at	with
from	by	up
over	to	of
beside	around	on
against	under	

2   Make up short sentences using each of these seventeen words as a preposition. You can use more than one word in the same sentence, if you wish.

3   The following prepositions, and the remainder of their phrases, are taken from the article 'How to survive a bushfire'. Pair each preposition correctly with the remainder of its phrase.

PREPOSITION	REST OF PHRASE
(a) from	safe times
(b) towards	the reach
(c) of	windows and ventilators
(d) during	the next few hours
(e) in	gutters
(f) to	flying embers
(g) at	your home
(h) for	a danger area

4   Pick out both the **prepositions** in each of these sentences, and also the **noun** (or **pronoun**) which is the object of the preposition.
   (a)   If there are fires in your area, shut all windows and doors.
   (b)   Most house fires are started under or inside the roof by flying sparks, so keep a ladder close to a manhole in your ceiling.
   (c)   Block downpipes with tennis balls and fill your guttering with water.
   (d)   Have your garden hoses connected, and make sure they reach beyond boundary fences.
   (e)   Don't put furniture out in the street.

(f) You are not covered by insurance if your furniture is outside.

(g) Lie down on the floor of the car with all the windows and doors closed, and preferably with a blanket or coat covering you.

(h) A roaring blaze will take 90 seconds to pass, and your chances of survival in the great heat are much better inside the car.

(i) Should your children be at school during an outbreak of fire that is probably the safest spot for them.

(j) Buckets should be full of water during this time.

Which would you choose?

'*Under* the circumstances'   '*in* the circumstances'?

Well, when you know that 'circumstances' literally means 'things that surround', then 'in' is the most sensible preposition to use. If prepositions were always chosen according to commonsense, then it would certainly be 'in' and not 'under'. However, the fact is that prepositions are not chosen according to logic, or rules, but according to the way most people speak. The most common preposition for the example above is 'under'.

Remember, prepositions very often go with groups of words not because of logic, but because they have just been used with that particular group of words for a long time, so that the usage is now the accepted one.

5 Choose the commonly accepted preposition that fits into the following sentences:

(a) Prices like these are a bit [.....] the fence!

(b) She was decorated for courage and service [.....] the call of duty.

(c) His low scores seem to indicate that he is [.....] the hill as a batsman now.

(d) It's no use closing the stable door [.....] the horse has bolted.

(e) From his slurred speech you could tell he was slightly [.....] the weather.

(f)   Whenever someone else comes up with a good idea he jumps [.....] the bandwaggon.

(g)   While the manager was away, the staff tended to let things go [.....] the board a bit.

(h)   You can tell by her attractive looks that she takes [.....] her mother.

(i)   She is endowed [.....] all the ability needed to take her [.....] the top.

(j)   He bestowed his wealth generously [.....] all those [.....] need.

CHANGE-A-LETTER

6 Can you work the following out?

- Start with the first word in each group, and by changing just one letter create a new word to go on the next line.
- Change another letter to create another new word, and so on.
- The changes must work towards, and fit in with, the final word in each group.
- You must always use real words, not made-up ones. (Hint: You can also work back from the last word to the starting word.)

    The first one has been done for you.

(a) FOLD	(b) BRAND	(c) SHINE	(d) BILL
hold	.....	.....	.....
hole	blind	shore	.....
hale	.....	.....	help
SALE	SLINK	STORY	HEMP

(e) SHIRK	(f) WIND	(g) SNOW	(h) HALF
.....	.....	.....	.....
.....	.....	.....	.....
.....	.....	.....	.....
SPURS	HUNT	SPIT	MALT

(i) STUNT   (j) MISS

.....	.....
.....	.....
.....	.....
CLING	PORT

THE WRITE APPROACH

7 Look back over the way the article 'How to survive a bushfire' is written. When you think you've got the feel of it, put on your journalist's hat, sharpen your biro, and get ready for your next assignment! You've just been asked to write a 300–500 word article for a famous weekly magazine, on one of the following topics!

(a) Surfing with safety.

(b) Tips on how to handle a flood.

(c) Pet care — practical suggestions.

(d) Hints on effective study.

TALK TIME

8 Imagine that your house is on fire. All the people and pets have been brought to safety. Now you just have time to save three other things from inside the house. Share around the class on the three things *you* would choose, and tell why. (P.S. Don't forget to really *listen* to each other!)

9 Set up a class debate on the topic: 'That tragedy and disaster always bring out the best in human nature.'

Unit Seventeen: Leopard

Colonel Jim Corbett is famous as the man who stalked and killed many man-eating tigers and leopards in India, during the 1920s. The man-eating leopard was credited with 125 kills between 1918 and 1926.

The wrong killer

An hour after dark a succession of angry roars apprised us of the fact that the leopard was in the trap. Switching on the electric light, I saw the leopard rearing up with the trap dangling from his forelegs, and taking a hurried shot, my .450 bullet struck a link in the chain and severed it.

Freed from the peg the leopard went along the field in a series of great leaps, carrying the trap in front of him, followed up by the bullet from my left barrel, and two lethal bullets from Ibbotson's shotgun, all of which missed him. In trying to reload my rifle I displaced some part of the light, after which it refused to function.

Hearing the roars of the leopard and our four shots, the people in Rudraprayag bazaar, and in nearby villages, swarmed out of their houses carrying lanterns and pine-torches, and converged from all sides on the isolated house. Shouting to them to keep clear was of no avail, for they were making so much noise that they could not hear us; so while I climbed down the tree, taking my rifle with me — a hazardous proceeding in the dark — Ibbotson lit and pumped up the petrol lamp we had taken into the machan with us. Letting the lamp down to me on the end of a length of rope, Ibbotson joined me on the ground, and together we went in the direction the leopard had taken. Halfway along the field there was a hump caused by an outcrop of rock; this lump we approached, with Ibbotson holding the heavy lamp high above his head, while I walked by his side with rifle to shoulder. Beyond the hump was a little depression, and crouching down in this depression and facing us and growling, was the leopard. Within a few minutes of my bullet crashing into his head, we were surrounded by an excited crowd, who literally danced with joy round their long-dreaded enemy.

The animal that lay dead before me was an out-sized male leopard, who the previous night had tried to tear down a partition to get at a human being, and who had been shot in an area in which dozens of human beings had been killed, all good and sufficient reasons for assuming that he was the man-eater. But I could not make myself believe that he was the same animal I had seen the night I sat over the body of the woman. True, it had been a dark night and I had only vaguely seen the outline of the leopard; even so, I was convinced that the animal that was now being lashed to a pole by willing hands was not the man-eater.

JIM CORBETT, *The Man-Eating Leopard of Rudraprayag*

Check your understanding

1   The incident described here took place
   (a)   just before dawn.
   (b)   in the middle of the night.
   (c)   in the early evening.
   (d)   in the late afternoon.
2   Choose the word closest in meaning to the first word. Check the dictionary at the back for any words you are unsure about.
   (a)   apprised: opened, informed, surprised, mentioned.
   (b)   lethal: deadly, legal, chemical, dangerous.
   (c)   bazaar: strange, market, church, village.
   (d)   hazardous: easy, careful, worrying, dangerous.
3   (a)   Why was it normally dangerous climbing down at night from a machan (a high platform for shooting tigers)?
   (b)   What made it particularly dangerous on this occasion?

4 The villagers swarmed out of their houses because
   (a) they heard the men shout.
   (b) they saw the hunters' light.
   (c) they heard the leopard's cries and the men's shots.
   (d) they hoped the leopard would show up.

5 Find one word in the passage for each of the following.
   (a) taking the words in their usual sense
   (b) came together
   (c) divided

6 Why did the hunters shout at the villagers to try and keep them clear?

7 Why were the hunters unable to make the crowd quieten down?

8 What caused the leopard to stop his flight and turn and face the hunters?

9 Explain the tremendous joy of the people at the death of this leopard.

10 Why did Corbett have doubts that this was the dreaded man-eater of Rudraprayag?

CONJUNCTIONS — JOINING WORDS

A **conjunction** is a word that simply carries out the job of joining other words, or groups of words, together. A conjunction is a joining word. By far the most common conjunction is 'and', both in speech and writing.

   Here is 'and' doing its work as a conjunction, joining words, and groups of words from the passage above.

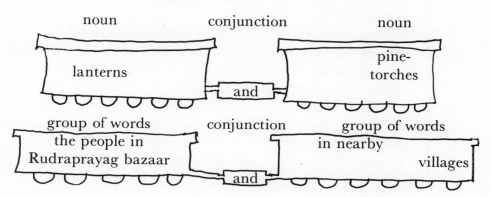

11   Complete the following common pairs each linked by 'and'.

(a) salt and .....   (b) bread and .....

(c) under and .....   (d) hundreds and .....

(e) here and .....   (f) fish and .....

(g) pen and .....   (h) meat pie and .....

(i) sweet and .....   (j) thunder and .....

(k) cup and .....   (l) bat and .....

(m) this and .....   (n) day and .....

(o) cat and .....   (p) sun and .....

(q) milk and .....   (r) cowboys and .....

12   Join the conjunction search! Look back over the passage, 'The Wrong Killer', and find the following sentences. Write out the sentence, and underline the conjunction.

(a) Where 'while' is used as a conjunction. [paragraph 3]

(b) Where two adjectives are joined by 'and'. [paragraph 4]

(c) In which two words *together* do the work of a conjunction. [paragraph 4]

(d) In which 'and' is used as a conjunction for the first time. [paragraph 1]

(e) Where two verbs are joined by 'and'. [paragraph 3]

(f) Which starts with a conjunction. (In this case the word is joining the ideas of this sentence to the ideas of the previous sentence.) [paragraph 4]

(g) In which two sounds are linked by 'and'. [paragraph 3]

(h) In which 'and' is used three times as a conjunction. [paragraph 3]

(i) Where 'so' is used as a conjunction. [paragraph 3]

(j) Where 'for' is used as a conjunction. [paragraph 3]

CONJUNCTION BOX

and   but   or   either . . . or   then   though   yet
since   whenever   wherever   while   because
however   for   if   until   although   where
after   unless   than   as
neither . . . nor

---

13   Use one of the conjunctions from the box to join the pairs of sentences together. Use a different conjunction each time. (Sometimes you will find it easiest to begin with your conjunction.)

(a)   The leopard had killed a cow. They decided to use the remains of the cow as bait.

(b)   Corbett and Ibbotson had to use all their strength to set the trap. The springs were so powerful they required two men to compress them.

(c)   The people were all terrified. The leopard was the cause of their terror.

(d)   Anyone who takes up hunting man-eaters must not be hasty. He must not be careless. (Use a pair of conjunctions!)

(e)   Corbett had an electric torch to help him make the shot. He was not all that keen on the troublesome piece of equipment.

(f)   Great care is needed in getting down from a machan with a loaded gun. This did not prevent Corbett from hurrying.

(g)   The villagers sat behind locked doors. Corbett and Ibbotson waited on the machan.

(h)   First Corbett descended from the machan. Ibbotson followed.

14   Complete the following sentences by building on from the conjunction.

(a)   A man does not know real fear **until** .....

(b)   The opportunity was there **so** .....

(c)   The two men sat **and** .....

(d)   They felt confident the leopard would come **although** .....

    (e)   Ibbotson held the lantern **while** .....
    (f)   The villagers felt safer **whenever** .....
    (g)   The man-eater was still alive **yet** .....
    (h)   Corbett would continue the hunt **after** .....

Warning

Over-use of conjunctions is a writing
(and speech) hazard!!!

Look at the following sentence.

> The hunt for the man-eater is a good story and I enjoyed reading
> it and I think everyone should try to read the book and I'm sure
> they would enjoy it, too.

Such a sentence is pretty boring (and tasteless) writing, simply because
the conjunction 'and' has been badly over-used. It would be much better broken into two sentences, to get away from the repetition of
'and'.

> The hunt for the man-eater is a good story and I enjoyed reading
> it. I think everyone should try to read the book, as I'm sure they
> would enjoy it, too.

15   Improve the following sentences by re-structuring them to avoid
the repetition of conjunctions.
    (a)   Tigers and leopards inhabit certain parts of India and usually
prey on other smaller animals and sometimes on cattle and
if they get very old and find it hard to hunt they sometimes
take to killing humans.
    (b)   Killers such as these will stalk their prey very carefully, then
silently move in, then make their kill, then drag the body off
into the jungle or some other part of the countryside.
    (c)   'These beasts can become very cunning, and er... you will
find they can often tell if a carcase has been poisoned as a
bait, and er... they won't even touch it.'

RHYMIN' SIMON

To play Rhymin' Simon, simply find the answers to the following clues. In each case the answer is a pair of rhyming words. The numbers in brackets after the clues will tell you how many letters each word has.

16 (a) Sick fowl (5,5)   Crook chook
       Away you go with the rest!
   (b) Cranky employer (5,4)
   (c) Crazy fashion (3,3)
   (d) Inexpensive woolly animal (5,5)
   (e) Pleasant Asian food (4,4)
   (f) Delicate garden pest (5,5)
   (g) Stupid friend (4,4)
   (h) Night-bird's cries (4,5)
   (i) Poor quality food between meals (5,5)
   (j) A big southpaw (5,5)
   (k) Equestrian marriage breakup (5,7)

PUNCTUATION

17 Punctuate the following, correctly.

three people stood before the judge on a charge of drunken disorderly conduct what were you doing the judge asked the first man just throwing peanuts in the lake the man replied what were you doing the judge asked the second man i was throwing peanuts in the lake too the man replied turning to the third man the judge asked and whats your story were you throwing peanuts in the lake too no your honour replied the third man i am peanuts

REDUNDANCY

Redundancy is saying the same thing twice with no good reason for the repetition.

The army *advanced forward* to meet the foe.

Since the word 'advanced' already contains the idea of 'forward', it is unnecessary to include the word 'forward' in the sentence. The redundancy would be corrected by simply removing 'forward' from the sentence.

The army advanced to meet the foe.

18 Correct the following sentences by removing any examples of redundancy.

    (a) The builder was working on some new renovations to the house.

    (b) It is just exactly ten years ago that the accident occurred.

    (c) His first initial reaction was one of disbelief.

    (d) There was a look of confused bewilderment on his face.

    (e) He is a master of insincere flattery.

    (f) Finally, to finish things off, I would like to thank you all for coming.

    (g) The bushranger was killed by a fatal shot from a gun.

    (h) When you are completely finished we can go.

    (i) The overseas ambassador was recalled back from his post.

    (j) The idea began originally in the writings of Shakespeare.

THE WRITE APPROACH

19 Write a composition around the following title, and situation.

Hunter, or Hunted?

You are a famous sportsman, responsible for hunting down many man-eaters. The Indian government has called you in to hunt down another man-eater — an aging, female tiger, who has acquired a taste for human flesh. As you lie in wait at night, near a recent kill, a storm begins to brew up. You suddenly realise that the noise of the rain will prevent you hearing if the tiger approaches, and that the rain itself will cut your vision.

    Here is the opening sentence of your composition. Continue, and tell what happens!

        My limbs were already trembling with the first shock of the cold water, but now the hair on the back of my neck began to prickle too, as I became aware of the danger I was in.

TALK TIME

20 Use the following themes as talking points for discussion in your class.

(c) The invention of gunpowder was a backward step for mankind.

(b) The only hunting that should ever be done is hunting for food, or to protect life.

(c) All guns in Australia should be registered so that police have a record of all gun-owners in the country.

Unit Eighteen: Daddy

Light gone all dark!

'Daddy! Light gone all dark!'

Light gone all dark.

'The bulb in her nightlamp's gone,' said Jack. 'The one you put in yesterday.'

Marvellous — the one I put in yesterday. 'I'll put in the one from the hall.'

'It's not there. I used it for the bathroom. To replace the one you used for your study.'

Musical lights. I had to go to the shops.

'If you buy one of these,' said the man producing a special one, 'it won't go bung so quick.'

I bore it home. 'I could only afford one,' I told them. 'But it won't go bung so quick.'

It didn't, either. That one lasted two days . . .

Why? How does it happen? It didn't happen in my father's day.

Lights didn't go bung then. What happened to the lights in my father's day was they got dusty — that was all.

Every two years or so you had to go to the bother of cleaning them. Then you bunged them back in, turned them on, and you were right for another two years.

But those were the good old days. Those were the days when electricity was still in its infancy, and *trying*.

Those were the days when a bulb was a bulb, sir, and not a transparent imitation.

Light at the flick of a switch? Lights that work?

Not now. Now I spend half my waking hours messing with lights. Like the other day: the kitchen one went, right in the middle of the gravy.

'I can't see!'

'Daddy! Mummy can't be seeing!'

'Plop,' said George.

I got out the one from the dining-room.

'Sumsing be touching me on my leg!' said S in the dark.

'Jooby-jooby,' said the toucher. It was George.

'Hurry up,' appealed Jack from the stove.

'You too slow,' complained Mrs S. 'Be running, please.'

I placed a child's chair without a back on top of a grownup's with a wonky leg and clambered up. Everything wavered.

'Hold my legs! My legs!'

'I can't. If I stop stirring, gravy'll end up all lumpy.'

That's all we needed: lumpy gravy.

'It's orright, daddy. I hold.'

'No!'

'I only trying help a bit.'

I managed to get it in, but sort of landed on a small body when I came down.

'Hey!' wailed George. But Mrs S explained that I hadn't meant it.

We ate with candles. It wasn't romantic because of the fumes, and they only lasted as far as the bread pudding.

'The light's going well in the kitchen.'

It was the one bright spot. I found some money and bought more like it the next day. The man said he had yet another kind which was perhaps better, but I was sticking to the one I knew.

It's silly changing lights. Especially when you've got to get up on chairs to do it.

CHARLES BOAG, *Woman's Day*

Check your understanding

1 Are the opening words spoken by a boy or a girl? Explain how you arrive at your answer.
2 Where had the light from the hall been re-located?
    (a) in the nightlamp?
    (b) in the study?
    (c) in the bathroom?
    (d) in the kitchen?
3 What was the only problem encountered with light bulbs in the 'good old days'?
4 Find words in the extract which mean:
    (a) able to be seen through, (b) childhood, (c) wobbly, (d) climbed with hands and feet.
5 Find *three* things about electricity and lights in the 'good old days' which were different from today.
6 Judging from their speech, identify the youngest member of the family. Give two examples of this person's speech.
7 'You too slow. Be running, please.' Why does Mrs S speak the way she does?
8 Why does Daddy not want his legs held by the child who offers?
9 Explain the two meanings of the sentences: 'It was the one bright spot.'
10 Explain in your own words the meaning of the following.
    (a) go bung
    (b) bunged it in
    (c) appealed
    (d) imitation

PARTS OF SPEECH — GENERAL REVISION

11 Identify the part of speech of each of the words in bold black type.

(a) '**Light** gone all dark!' (Answer — 'Light': common noun)
(b) I'll put **in** the one from the **hall**.
(c) It didn't happen in **my father's** day.
(d) **But** those were the good **old** days.
(e) Those were the days **when** electricity was still in **its infancy,** and trying.
(f) That's all we **needed: lumpy** gravy.
(g) The **light's** going **well** in the kitchen.

12 Now identify all the parts of speech in the sentence: **It was the one bright spot.**

A FURTHER REFRESHER COURSE

● Remember, a singular subject takes a singular verb, and a plural subject takes a plural verb.
● The following words are all singular, and take singular verbs.

each	either	neither	either . . . or
neither . . . nor	everyone	everything	everybody
someone	something	somebody	no one
nothing	nobody		

13 Choose the correct verb and write out the sentences.

(a) Everyone [was/were] keen to participate.
(b) The birds [is/are] beginning to migrate.
(c) Neither Sarah nor Felicity [has/have] been chosen for the part.
(d) Nothing [stand/stands] between us and victory in the game.
(e) Either of the girls [is/are] capable of taking the prize.
(f) The sketches of the ship [was/were] chosen to illustrate the book.
(g) Everybody [find/finds] that they are better at some subjects than others.
(h) We wondered whether anyone [was/were] prepared to take on the job.

THEIR, THERE, THEY'RE

'Their' is a pronoun . . . *their* house.

'There' is an adverb . . . over *there*.

'They're' is a contraction standing for 'they are' . . . *they're* talking.

14   Choose the correct word and write out the sentences.

    (a)   Most people prefer ..... clothes to be up with the fashions.

    (b)   ..... still arguing about ..... defeat.

    (c)   The bus runs right past .....

    (d)   ....., where the car is parked, is the spot where the accident occurred.

    (e)   I'm afraid ..... inclined to laugh at any other point of view other than ..... own.

    (f)   He drove the car ..... without any trouble at all.

    (g)   Put it .....

    (h)   You'll often find ..... sensitive about letting ..... possessions be borrowed.

    (i)   They left all ..... rubbish .....

    (j)   The police have said ..... will be a charge brought against ..... company.

PARTICIPLES

15   Join the following pairs of sentences into a single sentence by changing *one* of the verbs into a participle.

    (a)   The man was walking down the street. He tripped and broke his ankle. (Walking down the street, the man tripped and broke his ankle.)

    (b)   The man put a brand new light bulb in the socket. He switched on the power.

    (c)   The teacher entered the classroom. He proceeded to write on the blackboard.

    (d)   The winger left his position. He ran infield and tackled the centre head-on.

    (e)   The horse turned away from the stable door. It galloped to the end of the paddock.

    (f)   He surveyed the ruins before him. He broke down, and wept.

CONJUNCTIONS

16 Join the pairs of sentences by using a suitable conjunction.
  (a) The stage is set for a real showdown. It looks as though neither side will back down.
  (b) The horse was brought back to the enclosure. He had just won the race.
  (c) The sky was quite clear. The weather bureau had forecast storms.
  (d) The crowd was angry. The cause of their anger was the referee's poor decision.
  (e) She was unable to go herself. She gave her ticket to a friend.

PREPOSITIONS

17 Show that you understand how prepositions operate in a sentence, by using the following words as prepositions, in sentences of your own.
  (a) after (b) before (c) under (d) across (e) behind (f) around
18 Make up your own sentences using the word 'round'.
  (a) as a preposition   (b) as an adjective
  (c) as an adverb   (d) as a noun
  (e) as a verb

VOCABULARY

19 Find a single word for each phrase. The first letter has been given as a clue. Each dot stands for a missing letter.
  (a) to bring it to an end [t........]
  (b) to find the correct answer is [s....]
  (c) to make two things the same [e.......]
  (d) to make up incorrect information [f......]
  (e) to ship from one country to another [e.....]
  (f) to stand in place of someone else [s.........]
  (g) to set free [l.......]
  (h) to provide an artificial system for watering the land [i.......]
  (i) to divide according to race, sex, colour, or a similar quality [d..........]

THE WRITE APPROACH

Funny things can happen in a home!

20 Roasting dookey birds or changing light bulbs, every home has its funny moments! Recall the time something humorous happened at your place and describe the incident in 1½ to 2 pages of writing.

TALK TIME

21 Discuss the following themes in your class.
  (a) Well, what about it? Were people better off in the 'good old days'?
  (b) When a manufacturer deliberately makes his product so that it will wear out, or break, after a period of time, and so force people to buy a replacement, we call this 'planned obsolescence'. Is planned obsolescence being carried too far these days? How could we combat it?

Unit Nineteen: Write on!

Some ideas to get you writing . . . and enjoying it!

1 Actions speak louder than words! (Tell of an action, good or bad, which you felt told you more about that person than words could have.)
2 Stop the world, I want to get off!
3 The day my hero (heroine) smiled at me.
4 If I had one wish right now . . .
5 The place I go to to get away from it all. (A description.)
6 If I were prime minister for a day . . .
7 My most precious possession.
8 The unluckiest person I've met.
9 *My* crazy idea for making money! (Dream up your own idea!)
10 Dear Graham Kerr, I have a problem with my cooking.

11   My dream girl (or boy).

12   If I could build a school.

13   There are a few things I can't stand.

14   Me — ten years from now!

15   Pop song with a message. (Write about a favourite pop song of yours that has a message. Explain what you feel is good about the song, and what could be improved.)

16   Sometimes I feel like a blob!

17   Love makes the world go round.

18   Greed makes the world go round.

19   When I retire, I'll . . .

20   If my friends could see me now!

21   There's something no one else knows about me.

22   Trail-bike riding (surfing/bushwalking/whatever) — a taste of freedom!

23   A fractured fairy tale.

24   How I see the fashions for the year 2000.

25   The day the science lab blew up!

26   My family, and other animals.

27   My crazy kid brother.

28   My solution for pollution.

29   Small is beautiful.

30   I've learned to be firm with grandchildren.

31   Old age . . . the forgotten years.

32   My most exciting moment in sport.

33   Write your own story starting with: The wind blew steadily from the south and the chill night air bit through my clothes.

34   Write your own science fiction story, ending with: I knew I would never see them again.

35   The great Australian outdoors (I love it!).

36   My friend, the cat/dog/budgie/etc.

37   The day the robot escaped.

38   Starting again in a new country. (What you would like if *you* were a migrant.)

39   My previously unpublished ghost story.

40 There's more than one kind of dope. (A young person talks to adults about drugs.)

41 Keep off the grass! (The case against drugs.)

How would you know your kids were into dope, if you spend most nights in the pub on your way home?

42 A letter to a travel firm requesting information about an overseas tour.

43 Dear Mum, you'll never guess where I'm writing from . . .

44 Reflections on grief.

45 Happiness is . . .

46 Diary of a lone survivor.

47 My thoughts on caring for severely handicapped people.

48 A funny thing happened on the way to school.

49 A lesson I'll never forget!

50 The unluckiest person I've met.

51 The person I'd like to marry.

Unit Twenty: Dictionary

- Where a word has several possible meanings, the different meanings are numbered.
- Other forms of the words have been bracketed below the meaning.

abstract a very general idea (e.g. 'honesty'). Not concrete or material [abstraction]

absurd silly, ridiculous, funny [absurdity]

accelerate to speed up or make something go faster [accelerating, acceleration, accelerator]

accomplished (1) a task that is finished, (2) a clever or talented person, e.g. an accomplished musician [accomplish, accomplishment]

affect to bring about a change

ambassador a diplomatic officer sent to look after the affairs of his own country in another country

appalling terrifying, causing dismay [appalled]

apparent obvious [apparently]

assessment an estimation of the value [assess]

astringent harsh, severe

bestow give or confer something as a gift to someone

bitt a post on a boat to which ropes are tied

bizarre strange, fantastic

blissful full of happiness [bliss, blissfully]

blunder a stupid or careless mistake

boom (1) sudden business activity, (2) hum, roar, (3) a floating barrier across a harbour, (4) a pole stretching along the bottom of a sail

brunt the force of a blow, e.g. to bear the brunt of the attack

buffeted knocked, struck [buffet]

cameo a piece of raised carving in stone against a coloured background

capacity (1) capability, ability, mental grasp, (2) room, a space that can be filled

civilian a non-military person

clump (1) a group or cluster of trees or bushes, (2) the treading sound made by heavy boots

communication the exchange of knowledge or information

competence the ability to do something [competent, competently]

compress (1) squeeze together, (2) a pad applied to a wound, or injury [compression, compressible]

concise brief, short, to the point [concisely, conciseness]

confident fairly sure of success [confidently, confidence]

contend (1) to hold firmly to an opinion (2) to fight or struggle [contention, contentious]

continual always going on [continue, continually, continuation, continuing]

contorted twisted out of its normal shape [contort, contortion, contortionist]

convulsive a sudden, uncontrollable shaking [convulse, convulsion, convulsively]

cosmetic a substance designed to beautify hair, skin, complexion

debris scattered fragments, wreckage

denote stand, for, or show

depict to picture or describe in words or drawing

depleted emptied, used up

deprive take away [deprived, deprivation]

desperation a reckless, almost hopeless feeling [desperate, desperately]

discretion giving careful consideration to any thought or action [discreet, discreetly]

disposition the character or nature of a person

distinguish divide into groups or classes, see a difference

dorsal fixed on the back

effect (1) a result, e.g. one effect of the strike was a rise in wages, (2) to cause something to happen, to bring about, e.g. the doctors were able to effect a cure

effective successful in bringing about an effect

emotion feeling

enclosure a space that is completely closed in [enclose]

endow (1) to bequeath (in a will), (2) give as a gift, e.g. endowed with a talent for painting [endowment]

equestrian to do with horse-riding

excessive more than enough, too much [excess, excessively]

exhausted tired out [exhaust, exhaustion]

experiencing living, feeling and undergoing things [experience, experienced]

expertise special skill or knowledge [expert]

extract (1) remove, take out, (2) something removed or taken out, e.g. a passage from a book [extraction]

extreme (1) 'way out' in the sense of being unusual or strange, (2) very great [extremely, extremist, extremity]

fantasy imaginary scene [fantasia, fantastic]

forfeit give up, lose, pay as a penalty

fractured broken

fuselage the body of an aeroplane

futile useless [futility]

grimace this is made when you pull a face — especially one that's half puzzled, half funny. To grimace is to pull such a face

guarantee a pledge

habitually done as a habit [habitual]

hygienic clean and healthy [hygiene]

identifies when a person thinks of himself or herself as somebody else [identify]

impulse a sudden desire to act [impulsive]

incentive something given to encourage action, something that motivates

incredibly unbelievably [incredible]

infectious transmitting disease

initial at the beginning, coming first

inoculated given an injection of a mild form of a disease to prevent a violent attack [inoculate, inoculation]

insignificant small, unimportant, hardly worth noticing

interminable going on and on, seemingly endless

jargon very technical language. Any job or hobby has a special collection of words and phrases, e.g. 'hanging ten' in surfing

jaunty lively, cheerful, full of life [jauntiness]

jeer to mock or laugh at

keel the lowest timber on which a ship is built

knead to squeeze and mould dough

knoll a small rounded hill

laboured moved with difficulty, rolled and pitched heavily

lapse a slip of memory, or a slip of the tongue or pen, a slight mistake

literate able to read and write

local belonging to, existing in, or peculiar to a certain place [locality]

macabre gruesome, ghastly

malicious getting spiteful pleasure out of someone else's misfortune

manipulated handled, treated, dealt with skilfully [manipulate, manipulation]

massive huge and heavy

migrate to move from one country to another [migrant]

negligible of little importance

neigh the sound a horse makes

nevertheless in spite of that or in spite of everything

nonchalance lack of excitement, indifference, coolness (of spirit or feelings)

obsolescence the state of being out of date or going out of use [obsolescent, obsolete]

officiously attending to something in an interfering or meddlesome way [officious]

offset counterbalanced or compensated, e.g. food prices were offset by wage rises

ominously giving warning of evil to come, threatening [ominous]

onslaught a violent attack

orbiting circling

pacifier (1) peacemaker, (2) baby's dummy [pacify, pacifist]

partial (1) not whole or complete, incomplete, e.g. the excursion was only a partial success, (2) having a fondness or liking for something, e.g. they were partial to chocolates

participate take part in, have a share in [participation, participating, participant]

pectorals the fins on or near a fish's breast [pectoral]

peering looking closely or carefully at something [peer]

periodically going on from time to time, e.g. the kitten returned periodically for a sip of milk [period]

perishable able to be destroyed, subject to· decay, liable to perish, e.g. perishable items such as fruit and vegetables

personality (1) the special things or qualities that make you an individual person; your character, (2) a well known person, e.g. a TV personality

petite small, dainty

pioneer the beginner of an enterprise

placid calm and peaceful [placidly]

prejudice forming an opinion before knowing all the facts, bias against someone or something, or in favour of someone or something [prejudiced]

prey animal hunted by another for food

prime (1) coming first and being most important, (2) in excellent condition, e.g. prime beef, (3) in full health and strength, e.g. in her prime

profession occupation, vocation, calling — especially one in which a lot of skill, learning and experience is needed [professional]

proportion the proper balance or relation between various connected things or parts [proportional]

prosperous successful [prosperity, prosperously]

protruding sticking out [protrusion]

psychedelic vivid and dreamlike colours and shapes

qualify to take certain steps, e.g. passing exams, to fit you for a certain job or position [qualify, qualification]

qualm a sudden feeling of doubt

quarterly something that occurs or is due every quarter of a year

quay a wharf

queue a line of people waiting, e.g. to board a bus

quiet undisturbed, with little or no noise [quietly]

quite completely, altogether

raked (1) swept with bullets, shot, etc., (2) scraped or gathered together with a rake, (3) the swift-looking or streamlined backward slope of a plane's wings, a ship's masts, etc.

resents (1) to feel bitter or angry about an insult, (2) to feel jealous about someone or something [resentful, resentment]

salvo the firing of a number of guns all at the same time

sapling a young tree

scythe a cutting tool with a long, curved blade

self-sufficient having complete confidence in yourself, needing nothing from anyone else [self-sufficiency]

sensitive (1) readily responding to slight changes in conditions, (2) easily upset by criticism [sensitivity, sensitiveness]

sequence a connected series of happenings or events

situation (1) a place or position, (2) a job

skiff a small, light boat

slipstream the stream of air driven astern by a plane's propeller

soliloquy talking aloud to yourself with no one else present

solitary alone

specify to mention definitely or particularly

stifled choked [stifling, stifle]

stress strain, tension

summoned called [summon]

supreme highest in authority or rank [supremacy]

susceptible liable to, sensitive to [susceptibility]

synthetic artificial [synthesize]

technique method or skill

temporary lasting only for a short time

tenacious (1) clinging on, holding on fast, (2) stubborn [tenacity]

tethered tied up

tingles prickling, stinging

tire become weary or fatigued [tiresome]

toll (1) a tax especially for using a road or bridge, (2) casualties, e.g. road toll, (3) to make a bell ring slowly at regular intervals

torso the human trunk or body apart from the head and limbs, e.g. as in part of a statue

tottered walked unsteadily [totter]

transformed changed shape or character or feelings, e.g. after a holiday, they felt transformed and ready for anything [transform, transformation]

transparent easily seen through [transparency]

tuition instruction, teaching [tutor]

uneventful when nothing exciting happens

unscathed unhurt, not damaged

upholstery furniture which has been padded and covered with textiles, usually with springs

utilize to use or make use of [utilization, utility]

vain (1) to be too proud of or overwhelmed by your own appearance, (2) unsuccessful, e.g. she tried in vain [vanity]

variation any change or alteration [vary, variable]

wrenched pulled violently [wrench]

wistfully longingly, to think sadly or yearningly about someone or something [wistful, wistfulness]

yearn to long for someone or something [yearningly, yearning]

yoga a Hindu method of thinking, exercising and living which purifies the soul

yoghurt a food made from sour milk

zest enjoyment, interest, keen appreciation

DICTIONARY EXERCISES

1   The following three groups of words from the dictionary have been shuffled very unalphabetically! Try putting them back into alphabetical order.

- Look carefully at the second, third and even the fourth and fifth letters in words. ('Competence' comes before 'compress' because 'e' comes before 'r'.)
- As you sort out the words alphabetically, list them *down* the page — as the words are to be found in the dictionary.
- When you've finished, check your answer by looking up the groups of words in the dictionary.
  - (a) clump, confident, contend, cameo, contorted, cosmetic, civilian, communication, compress, continual, competence, capacity, convulsive, concise
  - (b) profession, pectorals, peering, participate, prey, pacifier, prime, placid, psychedelic, pioneer, protruding, prejudice, personality, partial, prosperous, perishable, proportion, periodically
  - (c) slipstream, sensitive, stress, skiff, sequence, solitary, situation, specify, salvo, summoned, stifled, self-sufficient, supreme, scythe, sapling, soliloquy, susceptible, synthetic

2 Answer each of the following questions.

- Look up the words in bold black type in the dictionary.
- Take one or more words from the meaning for your answer.

  Question: Give two other words that have similar meanings to **stress.**

  Answer: strain, tension.

(a) What animal are you dealing with when you use the word **equestrian**?

(b) What is driven astern in a **slipstream**?

(c) What are we thinking about when we talk about a person's **disposition**?

(d) Write down three other words that mean **absurd**.

(e) The word starting with 'o' that means **apparent**?

(f) **Keel** is linked with what kind of travel?

(g) Being **solitary** means being .....?

(h) **Quarterly** is linked with 'year'. Explain how.

(i) A **qualm** is a sudden feeling of .....?

(j) If you're **literate** you're able to [r.....] and [w.....].

(k) [H.....] and [s.....] — as **astringent** as that!

(l) Where on a fish's body would you find a **dorsal** fin?

(m) Where would you find the **pectorals**?

(n) **Macabre** is something that is ghastly and [g.....].

(o) What kind of an attack is an **onslaught**?

(p) What word would you put in front of 'importance' to describe **negligible**?

(q) A **pacifier** can also be described as a [p.....]

(r) How does a **grimace** differ from a guarantee?

(s) **Clump** has something to do with both 'trees' and 'boots'. Explain.

(t) Glass is **transparent** because it's [.....] through.

(u) Another word that has the same meaning as **incredibly**.

(v) If something is **futile** it is [.....less].

(w) What is a word starting with 's' that means **prosperous**?

(x) **Habitually means** [.....].

(y) What does an **incentive** encourage?

3 Words and meanings have gone haywire below! Have a go at linking up words and meanings correctly. When you've finished, check your answers in the dictionary.

(a)	**quite**	enjoyment, interest, keen appreciation
(b)	**quiet**	vivid and dreamlike colours and shapes
(c)	**yearn**	undisturbed, with little or no noise
(d)	**zest**	give or confer something as a gift
(e)	**summoned**	to long for something
(f)	**psychedelic**	completely, altogether
(g)	**synthetic**	stand for or show
(h)	**skiff**	called
(i)	**denote**	artificial
(j)	**bestow**	a small, light boat